Trucks, Buses, Planes & Tr

By

Derek J Rogerson

Foreword

This is my story – From 1952 until 2002 I worked in the manufacturing industry as an engineer for a variety of companies and in various positions. Whether by coincidence or choice I'm not to sure, but it transpires that all my places of employment were in the 'People Moving' field, hence the title of the book 'Trucks, Buses, Planes and Trains. All the people mentioned are real and all the names and events listed are as accurate as an ageing mind can recall. If however, when reading through these pages, you come across a name or event that does not ring entirely true then may I suggest that you keep the finding to yourself and be grateful that you have been blessed with a more judicious power of recollection than me. – Happy reading!

BOOK 1 – TRUCKS

Chapter 1 – Early Days

Chapter 2 – First Introductions

Chapter 3 – An Industrial Baptism

Chapter 4 – Off To College

Chapter 5 – Early Comet Capers

Chapter 6 – Life In The 'Pen'

Chapter 7 – First Placement

Chapter 8 – Among The Elite

Chapter 9 – National Service – Or Not?

Chapter 10 – Return to 104

Chapter 11 – Machine Shop Shenanigans

Chapter 12 – Time For A Break – The Ball

Chapter 13 – Another Break – Sports Day

Chapter 14 – A Seaside Break

Chapter 15 – Shop Trips & Cabarets

Chapter 16 - Climbing Up The Ladder

Chapter 17 – Blue Collar Days

Chapter 18 – I Join The 'Enemy' Ranks

Chapter 19 – North Works – The Magnet

Chapter 20 – The Headless Wonder

Chapter 21 – 'Howzat' – Shop Competitions

Chapter 22 – Climbing The Ladder

Chapter 23 – And The Winner is…

Chapter 24 – The 'A' Team

Chapter 25 – The Times They Are A-Changing

Chapter 26 – To The Manor Borne

Chapter 27 – Back To The Coal Face

Chapter 28 – Crosby To The Rescue

Chapter 29 – MRP II – We Need You

Chapter 30 – The Show Goes On

Chapter 31 – Shocking News

Chapter 32 – The Final Farewell

BOOK 2 – BUSES

Chapter 1 – Full Circle

BOOK 3 – PLANES

Chapter 1 – Ready For Take-Off

Chapter 2 – In The Shadow of Pendle

Chapter 3 – A Change of Direction

BOOK 4 - TRAINS

Chapter 1 – Final Journey

Chapter 2 – Hampsfield House

Chapter 3 – A Walk On The Fell

Chapter 4 – Back To Reality

Chapter 5 – And The Axe Fell - Again

Chapter 6 – Reprieved

FINAL CHAPTER

Comrades Still

BOOK 1

Chapter 1 – 1952 - Early Days

'Thar a bit early for school today Derek! Hast tha' wet thi bed?' chided Mrs Green as I passed her front door that fateful sunny morning in early August 1952?

'I'm not going to school today Mrs Green – I'm going to work,' I answered proudly. '

'Nay! I don't believe it. It weren't that long ago thi mam were pushing thi round in thi pram and then thar wer running around in short pants - and now thar gewing to work. Where ista gewing to work?' she asked with typical northern nosiness.

'Am going to be an apprentice electrician at t'motors,' I responded. Now everyone who lived within a twenty mile radius of the small Lancashire town of Leyland would have known exactly where I was about to start serving my time. T'motors, as it was more familiarly known as by us locals, was of course the world-famous Leyland

Motors and one of the nation's leading manufacturers of trucks and buses and at that time one of the largest industrial employers in the Northwest of the country.

I had received the acceptance letter about two weeks earlier, along with similar missives from other major employers in the area including the Electricity and Gas boards, Dorman Smiths and also the English Electric Company. It's true to say that there were few problems in the 1950's for school leavers wanting to take up apprenticeships in Industry. Order books at most manufacturing companies were bulging and any young lad with a leaning to engineering could almost be guaranteed an offer of apprenticeship.

It was quite a dilemma I can tell you, pouring over those acceptance letters. My initial choice was English Electric, whose two massive factories in Strand Road, Preston were making diesel and electric trains both for the home market and export. Not that that was the main consideration of this naïve 15 year old, more the fact that Strand Road was in walking distance of where we lived in South Meadow Lane and there would be no buses or trains to catch to get to work. Dad, however, had other ideas. He had lost out on a potential legal career, having started his working life as an articled clerk in a solicitor's office in Hawkshead, after matriculating with honours from Windermere Grammar School in the Lake District. This of course was in the 'Hungry Thirties' and as the depression deepened, his employers had to reluctantly let him go. Finding work of any kind in England was difficult at this time and, apart from farm labouring, virtually impossible in rural areas.

So with a wife and a six-month old baby (me), he decided to seek his fortune elsewhere and thus made the relatively short trip to Preston from Near Sawrey in the Lake District, once the home of a slightly more famous resident; the children's author and illustrator, Beatrice Potter for whom my grandmother was housekeeper for over 30 years – but that's another story in itself. Dad was pragmatic enough to realise that any hopes of resuming his legal career was as likely as finding the streets of Preston paved with gold. He was indeed thankful to take up any position that offered him a reasonable challenge and decent wages and so became a Production Liaison Officer or 'Chaser', as the position was colloquially known, at a small marine engineering concern called 'Freidenthalls'.

Having seen his future career path cruelly torn up, Dad was determined that I should not be faced with such disappointments. Unfortunately I had not at this stage in my life inherited his 'brains', so as a past scholar from St Stephen's C of E Primary School, and though not 'thick', I knew there would be no professional career for me. Thus at the tender age of 15 and with a boy's curiosity for all things electrical and mechanical, I was more than happy to pledge my allegiance to the world of engineering.

Dad and I mulled over those acceptance letters for many an hour, until with a sharp but street-wise wisdom, honed by earlier disappointments, he eventually and with great solemnity proclaimed that Leyland Motors should be my chosen employer. My initial disenchantment at his decision must have been plain to observe as I asked him how he had arrived at this decision. Now I'm not sure if dad had acquired the gift of second sight; had been looking over the shoulder of a certain Dr Beeching as he drafted his future transport plans or was just plain lucky with his reasoning but he reckoned that the nation was standing on the threshold of increased transportation by road and that the railroad's days were numbered - and to a point he was right.

"But dad," I pleaded desperately. "I'll have to catch a bus every day to Leyland."

"You could always go on your bike," was his response. "It's only 5 miles down the road and the exercise will do you good as well." - And so the die for the next 38 years or so was well and truly cast.

Chapter 2 – First Introductions

As I passed under the large ornate sign that declared that this was LEYLAND MOTORS Ltd for that very first time, little did I realize then that this would be just the first of many thousand such entrances over the next four decades. Along with a dozen or so other nervous new starters, we passed from the bright sunshine of a cloudless August day into the murkiness of what we later learned was the NORTH WORKS, the original Leyland Motors factory, to commence our induction tour. It was at this juncture that I began to wonder if dad and I had made the right decision.

These doubts were further reinforced as our apprehensive little party advanced down the central passageway of the factory to the accompaniment of weird metallic sounds and pungent odours that invaded our senses from the various workshops that we passed leading off from the main thoroughfare. To the left was the Nozzle Shop where the injector nozzles for all the family of Leyland engines were manufactured. This department was quite unique in the fact that it was 'manned' entirely by women. In this all female preserve, the only males to be found were the foreman, a couple of machine tool setters and a handful of apprentices. We later learned that as an apprentice, to be placed in the Nozzle Shop was quite an experience, particularly on Shrove Tuesday when by tradition apprentices were given a half day's holiday – But not to be enjoyed until the likewise tradition of being 'blacked up.' This usually involved having the face covered with black and evil smelling grunge and made to leave the factory looking like escapees from the Black & White Minstrel Show. However, the ladies of the Nozzle Shop had other ideas as to where the 'blacking' should be applied – But I think that propriety, so early in my story, bids that I quickly draw a veil over the exact anatomical site of its application.

On the right was 100 Department, a general machine shop consisting of mainly lathes of various types and sizes. Next door was 102, again a machine shop with a variety of grinding machines. Facing 102 was 105 Department, which consisted mainly of a variety of milling and drilling machines. On the opposite side again was the entrance to the Tool Room where the crème de la crème of engineers practised their highly skilled craft. Adjoining was the Heat Treatment Department where metal components were treated in furnaces before and after machining. Yet again on the facing side was probably the biggest and noisiest of the machine shops in the North Works, the combined 103 and 104 Departments. Here could be found all manner of metal shaping machines but predominantly lathes and where nearly all apprentice turners were destined to serve at least part of their apprenticeships.

It was therefore somewhat surprising when we encountered our first actual workers, for despite the gloom, the noise and the smell the majority seemed reasonably happy in what to us tenderfoots was a completely alien environment. Our tour continued around the various departments accompanied by much cheery and hearty banter from the workforce, which raised our spirits to the point that the more optimistic of the group were beginning to realize that working for a living was not going to be so bad after all.

At the conclusion of the North Works factory tour we were then shepherded across the busy main road to the factory complex known as the South Works. There we were taken to a sizeable building that we later learned was the Apprentices Training Centre and our first meeting with Harry Glassbrook, who at this time presided over all the young workers. Now Harry, apart from his engineering background was also an ex-army major and true to type he sported the perfunctory moustache that was considered de rigueur for such a British military rank. We sat down in rows and Harry, with his mock estuarine accent, delivered his somewhat long-winded welcoming speech. It was totally forgettable except for two things; his reminder that at this stage of our employment we were only employed as probationary apprentices and that it would take six months of hard work and application to show that we were fit to become engineers. Secondly his rather patronizing closing remarks, which were along the lines of, *'So remember boys, while you are at Leyland Motors – Let me be your father.'* An utterance that brought a number of stifled titters from the youthful assembly but nevertheless the sentiment and sincerity with which it was delivered struck home and those words will no doubt remain in my memory forever. However, it should not surprise anyone to learn that from that first meeting with Harry, he would forever be known, at least by our particular intake of youthful charges, as 'Dad'.

Later in his career with the company, Harry was appointed as 'House Father' at the company residence known as Wellington House. This imposing Victorian building was a 'home from home' for the 'Premiums' or elite young employees that had come into the company either direct from a university or college background or were well connected in the international motor or allied trades and usually from affluent families who could afford the cost or 'premium' for a specialised training outside the remit of a normal apprenticeship. Such privileged placement would virtually guarantee advancement within the company ranks to either specialized engineering or other high-flying managerial positions. However, by the late 1950's the premium structure was replaced by a less elitist system and though young men continued to be domiciled at Wellington House they were now known as Student Apprentices.

Despite his military background, Harry was looked on by many of his charges as a bit of a 'soft touch' and was very often the butt of many inane pranks and practical jokes. The one I remember best was when a group of the more enterprising students managed to park his little sports car, not in the garage of his adjoining bungalow but actually on top of it. How they managed this remarkable feat is a secret to this very day. There was also **the unconfirmed tale of probably the same group of students** dismantling and then rebuilding one of Harry's cars inside his lounge and then bricking up the window afterwards – But I digress…

It was at this juncture back in the Training Centre that things took on a more serious aspect as Harry introduced us to Mr Darnell, who we learned was the Head of the company's own technical college. He was quite a serious and rather forbidding figure as he questioned each of us on our scholastic achievements over the previous ten years or so. We later learned that this was part of the streaming exercise to ascertain at what level we should commence our academic engineering education. Even at this early stage of our employment, the company were keen to establish who would be the future shop floor workers and who were destined for the more prestigious jobs such as draughtsmen, planning engineers and the like. As a lowly primary school pupil I was placed with the majority of the lads in the former stream and was informed that I would be starting on the Preliminary Technical Course, which would eventually lead to the City & Guilds Certificate, a qualification best suited for the more practical engineer. The few remaining ex-grammar school and Technical College graduates were told that they would be starting on the Preparatory National Certificate course, an educational avenue that would eventually lead them to more design and development based honours. What we didn't know at that time was that these preliminary decisions were not set on tablets of stone and that any scholar initially enrolled on the more practical course that showed ability had indeed the opportunity to 'change ship'. This in fact is what happened to me – but that's a story for a later Chapter.

Chapter 3 – An Industrial Babtism

Our future education now mapped out, we were sent home early on that first day with strict instructions to report to the Apprentices Training Centre at 7-30am sharp the following day. From there we would be assigned to our work places for the next three months or so. Three months did I hear someone say? I thought apprentice training took six years or so? And so it did, however the Leyland motors system was ahead of its time in the way they introduced their young men to the concept of working by giving them 'tasters' in all aspects of manufacturing in three monthly slots. This gave the tenderfoot engineer the opportunity to discover first hand what they were good at. The system clearly worked as I for one, who originally had dreams of being an electrician, soon realized that my true vocation lay elsewhere…

The aroma of frying bacon woke me at 6-00am the following morning and as I hurried downstairs it was to find mum preparing me a hearty breakfast 'to set you up for the day' as she put it. Trixie, our family dog appeared puzzled. She was clearly not used to there being so much activity in the household at such a godforsaken hour. However, bacon and eggs consumed and my 'bagging' tin tucked under my arm, she gave my hand a friendly lick of encouragement as I left the house on a journey that I was to repeat almost daily for the next four decades.

At 7-30am prompt, we stood in a nervous little group as the Training Centre supervisor assigned each of that morning's intake to their various work places. "And you Rogerson will be working in the South Works Inspection department," he announced handing me various documents including my 'clocking on' card. "And as we are in the South Works now, you will not have far to travel. Right off you go and report to Mr Cheetham the Inspection Superintendent and he will tell you which 'shop' you will be working in." I eventually found my way to Mr Cheetham's office and there a tall, stout, silver haired gentleman greeted me most affably. He invited me to sit down, sent his secretary out to make me a 'brew' and then told me what was expected of me whilst I worked in his little empire.

Pleasantries completed he then gave me a tour of the South Works where I learned that this was the bus body making plant and consisted of all aspects of sheet metal working and joinery. I was somewhat alarmed as we passed through the assembly section as the noise from the dozens of riveting guns was quite deafening. Fortunately the inspection area that I was to work in was situated in a quieter part of the factory and it was there that I first met the man who initially scared me to death but ultimately turned out to be a great inspiration in my early days as a prospective engineer – Jack Griffin, the section foreman.

Mr Griffin explained to me what my main duties would be for the next few weeks or so. Initially I was to be the department's 'gofer'. That meant that I had to go for all the tools, gauges, drawings etc that the dozen or so inspectors required in order to check the quality of the work produced by the various manufacturing sections. However, the inspection staff had a totally different concept of what my main duty was and this of course was as the section 'brew boy'. This most important task consisted of carrying a tray, almost as big as me, filled with cups, mugs and brew cans to the hot water station at least three times a day. There, along with other similarly appointed apprentices, I would fill up the various ceramic and tin receptacles and return to the section with hot steaming beverages, the consumption of which no doubt helped enormously in keeping the wheels of industry turning. When Fridays came round, most of the guys would slip me a 'three penny bit' or the more generous ones a 'tanner'. Now this may not seem much but on a starting wage of 29 shillings a week (about £1.45 in today's currency), most of which was handed over to mum, it turned out to be quite a worthwhile supplement to my 'five bob' weekly pocket money – However, let me tell you how I finished up earning more from my domestic duties than Leyland Motors was paying me as an apprentice engineer.

Within a couple of weeks I had expanded my 'brewing up' empire quite considerably. I discovered that there were little pockets of workers who did not enjoy the services of a brew boy and who were quite pleased when I offered to perform this task for them in return for a small fee each week. This quickly escalated into me actually providing the ingredients for the various beverages for which I felt justified in charging each customer half-a-crown (12.5p) per week. The guys were more than happy with this arrangement and it continued for the best part of a couple of months – And then my little moneymaking enterprise collapsed at a stroke. It was a Monday morning when Mr Griffin strode into the department with a young boy who was obviously as nervous as I had been on my first day. He escorted him over to my little corner where I was diligently preparing the big tray for the first brew of the day.

"Leave that Derek, you've been promoted," he announced. "No more running round for tools and gauges for you my lad, I'm putting you with Fred Sumner our sample inspector in the press shop. There you will help Fred with the actual 'first off' checks, and best of all you will not have to worry about brewing up for the lads anymore, young Martin 'ere will be taking on that job" – I could have cried!   Still, it had been good while it had lasted, but I was philosopher enough to realize that it couldn't go on forever. I smiled as appreciatively as I could at Mr Griffin as I grudgingly handed over my little money spinning empire to Martin.

My time with Fred proved most interesting and under his guidance I learned much about all aspects of sheet metal working. I believe it was at this point where I first questioned my decision to become an electrician. The manufacturing process of the various parts that went to make up a vehicle intrigued me, whether they be for a bus or a truck it mattered little, I began to really appreciate seeing things take on various intricate shapes and forms from previously nondescript metal sheets. Jack Griffin noticed my growing enthusiasm for the art of metal shaping and during my final weeks in the department entrusted me with more and more responsible tasks – But then came that fateful day when my unbounded enthusiasm was shaken to the core…

It was a week or so before the Christmas of 1952 and everyone was getting into the festive spirit when I first experienced the dark side of manufacturing. I was assisting Fred in checking a side frame when a piercing scream rose above the usual noisy atmosphere of the press shop. Within yards of where we were working a middle-aged guillotine operator staggered back from the operating pedal of his machine, clutching his hand and screaming both with pain and shock as to what had just happened to him. No doubt he had operated that pedal thousands of times in the past with no ill effects – But once – and that's all it takes - he let his concentration wander and the shear blade of the guillotine, having been given the appropriate signal, descended – and removed four of the poor guy's fingers. Fred dashed over and I instinctively followed – Oh God, how I wish I hadn't. The victim was staring in disbelief as he held up the stump of his hand. Like a bird hypnotized by the snake. I could not help but stare at this truly appalling sight – But where's the blood I thought – There was hardly any at that point and as his workmates crowded round him offering comfort and help, Fred placed his arm around my shoulder and led me away from the distressing tableau. Over my years at Leyland I was witness to a number of industrial accidents but none affected me as much as that first upsetting one. My previous growing desire to become a metal shaper was badly blunted that day. However, as with most unhappy episodes in life, time once again proved to be a great healer and the vision slowly faded in my memory. This sad little tale though had a reasonably satisfactory ending as the man who had that awful day been maimed for life eventually returned to work and was found a position that suited his infirmity and there he remained for the rest of his working life….

It was not long after the Christmas break when Mr Griffin informed me that I would be moving shortly to continue my training in the Comet Shop Tool Stores. The Comet Shop was situated in the Farington plant and had been so named, not surprisingly, as this was the dedicated factory where the famed Leyland Comet was manufactured. Apart from engine, bodywork and chassis, most other vehicle parts such as transmissions and axles was both manufactured and assembled under this massive roof – and massive it certainly was. It occupied the site, and more, where the Morrison superstore now stands, which will give you some idea as to just how much shop floor space the factory occupied. This was to be my first spell in the Comet Shop but it certainly wasn't the last, but steady on old chap - You're getting ahead of yourself - Those exploits are for a later chapter.

Chapter 4 – Off To College

If the new intake thought that schooling was finished now that overalls had been donned, well they were in for quite a surprise. Within a week or so of 'clocking on'

for the first time, we newly fledged apprentices were assigned to our various courses to be held at the companies own Technical College in Leyland. As I mentioned earlier my relatively basic educational background meant that I was to start on the PTC or Preliminary Technical Course. That first morning we assembled in the well-equipped Physical Training hall and were then introduced to the teachers who would be our guides and mentors for the duration of the course. The college 'Head', Mr Darnell, a rather stern taciturn man from the old school of teaching, performed the introductions. He was soft of voice but hard on discipline and certainly not a chap to get on the wrong side of so early into the game. After his initial opening remarks he then introduced us to Bill Preston, who was to take us for maths' and technical drawing; Viv Yeo, a ruddy faced Welshman who appeared to have left his sense of humour in the valleys and was to introduce us to the mysteries of science based subjects and last but by no means least, Tom Jones – No! Not that one, this particular Tom Jones was far more of an inspiration to me than he of the 'Voice' fame. This was the guy who would attempt to teach us budding engineers all aspects of the English language and it is he who I must thank for awakening in me my love of creative writing.

It was during those first few months at college that I realized just how academically 'thick' I was. Oh they had tried hard enough during my 10 years of full time schooling but somehow very little of the various subjects taught had appeared to stick in my head. Fortunately with this realization of inadequacy came a steely determination to turn things round and thanks to the skill and patience of the aforesaid tutors and my own resolve, I managed to pass the first year's exam' with enough marks to be moved on to the National Certificate Course.

It was during this second year that the Head, Mr Darnell, retired, to be replaced by an academic by the name of Harry Bailey whose claim to fame was that he had written a book on 'speed reading'. I recall well the one and only time he attempted to pass on this technique to some of the brighter students. To say it was a calamitous error would be to understate the attempt as the plain speaking Lancashire lads told him in no uncertain manner where he could stuff his theories. To be fair, he realized he was preaching to the wrong audience, quickly dropped all attempts to convert us all to speed reading and I'm glad to say became a good college head and eventually gained the respect of both pupils and tutors.

The next 5 years flew by and apart from one academic stumble along the path I was eventually awarded my National Certificate. I was sensible enough to realize I had probably reached the zenith of my scholarly ability and so bade a fond goodbye to the Halls of Academia. Besides there were other events that were threatening to take up my time. One wore a skirt and the other I would have to salute! – I'll tell you more in a subsequent chapter.

Chapter 5 – Early Comet Capers

The conclusion of chapter 3 found me leaving South Works to continue my probationary training in the Comet Shop. Stepping into the Comet Shop was like entering a whole new industrial world. South Works was more a collection of various small to mid-size buildings, each one allocated to a different manufacturing task, with separate workshops added over the years as the vehicle business expanded. The Comet Shop however was a totally different concept. Here was a huge custom built factory designed specifically to both manufacture and assemble many of the major units that went to make up the Comet family of trucks and buses. The very first vehicles to display the 'Comet' badge were launched in 1948 and over the next two decades or so the range expanded and benefited from a range of upgrades, culminating in the 'Super Comet' and remained a popular choice for many national and international truck and bus operators.

I was instructed to report to the Tool & Gauge Store foreman, a certain Mr E. E Vick, and of course thereby hung a tale. Speculation was rife as to what the second 'E' stood for. Of course everyone knew that the first initial was for Ernest or Ernie as he was more familiarly known, but that second 'E' had us all flummoxed. Many attempts were made to uncover the mystery and as far as I know nobody ever found out the true answer. However, and according to his second in command in the stores, at his christening, his godfather had such a bad stutter that when the vicar called, 'What names are given to this child?' he replied, 'E-e-ernest E-ernest – And his Parents loved him so much that they decided to stick with it. It could have been that a certain Gerard Kenny was around at the time and it gave him the inspiration for writing his one and only hit number – New York New York – So good they named it twice. Ernie was of that ilk and he revelled in the mystery surrounding that second 'E' and kept it a closely guarded secret until the day he retired.

I was one of three young apprentices seconded to the Tool & Gauge stores at that time and although our duties appeared to be mundane and repetitive, once again they gave us an insight as to how a large manufacturing company operates. Our job was to ensure that all gauges and measuring devices that were in use on the shop floor were accurate and calibrated correctly. This meant that periodically the equipment in use had to be changed – and that's where we came in. Equipped with a tray or a trolley filled with freshly calibrated instruments, we would visit all corners of the factory, picking up out of date equipment and exchanging it for new. While performing this work we naturally became familiar with all the different types of measuring devices and how they were applied. There were plug gauges for measuring holes; calliper gauges for measuring external diameters; thread gauges for measuring screwed parts and many, many more intricate and precise instruments for measuring any component part that required to be manufactured to a prescribed tolerance.

These trips around the factory also allowed us fledgling engineers to view first hand the infinite variety of machines that were required to make the component parts. There were various types of drilling and boring machines for creating holes; there were lathes, both large and small for making cylindrical parts; there were specialist type machines for the cutting and grinding of gear teeth, in fact depending on how material was required to be shaped or fashioned there was a machine designed to perform the task. It was on one of these gauge changing trips and whilst observing a young man not much older than myself, transforming a billet of shapeless steel on his lathe into a shining component that would eventually be fitted into a gearbox, that all previously held desires to become an electrician, a desire that had been waning for some time, deserted me totally, to be replaced by the trade that I was now determined and destined to follow – that of a Turner.

The manufacture of vehicle parts and ensuring that the correct equipment was available for the task was considered a serious business; yet there was always time for lighter moments. I remember well during my first week becoming a victim to the classic con' that has been played on young and naïve apprentices ever since the factory system was brought into being. Oh! I was mindful of the old glass hammer and rubber nails scenario and even the bucket of cold steam, but up to then the 'Long Stand' was not on my list of 'practical jokes to be aware of' – until that day. I was called over by one of the senior storekeepers and told that a 'Long Stand' had been wrongly delivered to one of the fitters in the gearbox assembly area and would I be a good lad and go and retrieve it. Eager to please I went to where I was directed and informed the fitter in question that I had come for the 'Long Stand'.

"Mmm! Now where did I put it?" he replied to my request. "Just wait there a minute sonny and I'll see if I can find it." Off he trotted and I stood there patiently waiting for his return. Five minutes passed and then ten. At the twenty-minute mark I began to feel concerned. After half-an-hour had passed and there was still no sign of the fitter or the long stand I reckoned it was time to return to base and report on the incident.

"Ah! I see you managed it OK then," announced the man who had sent me on the uncompleted mission. Of course I had to inform him of what had happened and that I had been unable to return with the 'Long Stand'. "How long were you there?" he enquired.

"Over thirty minutes," I informed him.

"Did you sit down at all?"

"Of course not," I responded.

"Well now that's what I call a good long stand." He replied, his face breaking out into a wicked grin. All the workers in the stores joined in the merriment - It was then that the penny finally dropped.

There was also another memorable moment regarding the exchange system for gauges that happened with one of the other apprentices that was working with me at the time. John (not his real name) had a slight accident as he was exchanging a calliper gauge one day – He dropped it. Feeling somewhat embarrassed but relieved that no one had observed the clumsy act, he exchanged it for the one to be re-calibrated. When he had exchanged all his gauges he returned to the stores to find the place in an uproar, with Ernie-Ernie and a distraught machinist going at it hammer and tongs.

"And I'm telling you it's not my fault," shouted the angry machinist, waving a large calliper gauge. "They were all spot on to the other gauge and now they're all undersize to this new one that the lad just brought – I'll get sacked for this when the foreman finds out." John paled visibly. He recognized both the machinist and the gauge – it was the one that he had so carelessly dropped earlier. However, he must have had some of George Washington's blood coursing through his veins as he immediately stepped into the fray and confessed as to what had happened. The silence that followed, as they say, was deafening. Poor John got the biggest dressing down imaginable from E-E and was close to tears. Fortunately there was a happy ending to this story as when the dust had settled and the right size gauge established, it was found that all the components previously manufactured were indeed within the prescribed tolerances, while those produced using the faulty gauge were oversize and could thus be salvaged. So in the end no harm was done and no production lost. However, the incident served to teach both 'John' and I a very salutary lesson that served us both well over the years to come.

Following on from a few weeks of successfully collecting and dispensing measuring equipment from the shop floor, I was moved into the actual gauge room itself. This was the engineering equivalent of hallowed ground as it was inside this temperature controlled inner sanctum where all the various types of gauges and other measuring equipment were checked for accuracy and re-calibrated as necessary. Here I learnt how to handle the near sacred equipment that was used to check the measuring devices that were used on the shop floor (hope you're following this). They were treated with great reverence by the inspectors who used them and at the end of the working day they were cleaned, oiled and wrapped very carefully before been boxed and locked away for the night.

After a couple of months or so in this absorbing environment, I was informed that my probation period was coming to a satisfactory conclusion and that I would shortly be moving into the Apprentices Training Centre or the 'Pen' as it had been informally dubbed by previous 'inmates'. There I would be hopefully assigned to serve my apprenticeship in the trade I had selected. However, there was to be a 'sting in the tail' of this process. It appeared that of the thirty or so young hopefuls who were assembled, that more than half had chosen to become electricians. Now if I tell you that to successfully operate a large manufacturing concern, as LM certainly was, a diversity of trades and occupations were required. It was therefore improbable that out of the whole six monthly apprentice intake that 50% of them would be required as 'leccies'. Fortunately, even though my preferred choice was still listed as 'electrician', I was more than happy to be informed that the quota for turners had not been filled and would I consider filling one of the vacancies – I gladly accepted – and so my course for the next 5 years or so was set.

Chapter 6 – Life in the 'Pen'

Our trades confirmed, the rest of the happy band of turners and I, were assigned to the tender care of Mr Beech, the Machinist Training Instructor, who had a desk adjacent to the office of the gentleman I have already mentioned in an earlier chapter, Harry Glassbrook, the then Apprentice Training Manager. I was assigned to an old fashioned lathe that was belt driven and after a short induction period was given my first job – making plain washers – a simple enough task but one that introduced me gently to the workings of the lathe.

During our induction we were shown where the ambulance or first-aid room was situated. I paid little attention to this information, as I had no intention of ever visiting the place; a foolish notion for a turner to hold, which I soon discovered the hard way. On my second day the inevitable happened. I cut my finger on the sharp edge of a washer that I had just produced. Not to seriously but bad enough to warrant a visit to the dreaded ambulance room. What a revelation! The attending nurse treated me as though I was royalty; bandaged my wound, sat me down and made me a cup of strong tea. It was almost worth the initial injury for the kind way I was cared for. The nurse in question retired a few months later and it was some years later before our paths crossed again. It was our first holiday abroad and as Margaret and I lazed around the hotel pool we were approached by an elderly lady who enquired, "Didn't you work at Leyland Motors?" To which I replied that I was still there. She smiled and continued, "You probably don't remember me but I bandaged your finger when you worked in the Training Centre." Now how's that for a happy coincidence?

There was a real sense of camaraderie in the 'pen' and many friendships were formed, some that are still alive and kicking despite the relentless passage of time. However, lads being lads their was also a fierce spirit of competition abroad. This manifested itself in many ways, none more so than during the lunch break when the various trade apprentices formed football teams in the winter and cricket 'elevens' in the summer. The yard outside the Training Centre, when the lunchtime buzzer sounded, was instantly transformed into either a football pitch or a cricket square, depending on the season and so intense was the rivalry that very often the 'start work' buzzer was not even heard, well that was the excuse we offered when either Mr Beech or one of his training colleagues came out to disrupt the game and drag us back inside.

But hang on! I can imagine many of you thinking, isn't lunchtime meant to be spent – well – having lunch? Technically you would be correct in this assumption but so keen was the spirit of competition that many of the eager combatants either ate their 'bagging' surreptitiously before the buzzer or missed it altogether. I have a feeling however that these little acts of deceit were well known to the management – they just chose to turn a blind eye to the practice as long as the work required was done.

This feeling was further reinforced when on a particular wet and windy day in high summer (a not uncommon feature in the grim northwest), a mini cricket field was set up in what we thought was a quiet corner of the workshop. It was my turn at the crease and I faced the first ball from a young guy who could hurl them down as speedily as any of the legendary West Indian fast bowlers that were around at that time. A lucky strike and the ball sped from my makeshift bat the full length of the workshop. The entire ensemble held its collective breath and gazed in horror as the high trajectory of the errant wallop carried it towards the large factory clock on the far wall – It missed by about a foot.

We were all thinking what a lucky escape when from out of his office, moustache fairly bristling, strode the Training Manager – Harry (let me be your father) Glassbrook. He reached first the unfortunate young man who had delivered the missile. Oh oh, thought the collective gathering, he's in for it now.
"SMITH," he hollered, "That was a no ball. You can't bend your arm like that and expect to get away with." Young Alex stood there totally stunned. It was certainly not the reaction he had been expecting. He then turned his attention in my direction. "As for you Rogerson, that was not a recognizable cricket stroke, it was more like an agricultural 'hoik'. You'll be caught at Long On every time with strokes like that. And besides, if that clock had been broken you'd all have to work until I said it was time to stop!" He then addressed the rest of the miscreants advising them to be a little

more discreet with their premature dining habits or there would be serious consequences. I've often wondered what that they would have been.

On the whole, we happy band of apprentices were a reasonably well-behaved and industrious lot. However, on the odd occasion testosterone would bubble to the surface and the odd punch would be thrown. For some reason these hostile acts always seemed to start in the foundry area adjacent to the main workshop. This was a small aluminium foundry, set up to teach future foundry workers the finer points of producing metal castings and all the ancillary activities demanded such as core and pattern making, sand moulding, die casting, dressing and cleaning. As well as the usual furnaces and workbenches, sand piles took up some of the floor space, a necessary constituent for the making of cores.

Arthur, an ex-foundry worker himself who appeared to know everything there was to know about this 'black art', ran the foundry and for those who have ever stepped over the threshold of a foundry, particularly one producing cast iron parts, then I'm sure they would agree that the terminology 'black art' is most apt. The place always reeked of hot fumes and burnt molasses and maybe it was this volatile atmosphere that had something to do with the occasional acts of aggression.

I recall one such event when an argument about nothing in particular got out of hand and pretty soon there were at least half-a-dozen young men going at it hammer and tongs. It was more handbags at dawn rather than actual fisticuffs except for one poor guy, a mere spectator I might add, and who was accidentally sent sprawling by an errant punch into one of the aforementioned sand piles. By the time he had gathered his senses and cleaned his glasses, an earlier shout of "look out lads" had caused the combatants and onlookers to disperse, he found himself eyeball to eyeball with – yes you've guessed it – the ubiquitous Harry Glassbrook.

Now whether it was something in his military background or not, but the one activity that Harry would not tolerate under any circumstances was fighting. Anyone caught engaging in this pursuit could expect at the least a period of suspension or for repeat offenders, dismissal. Despite his protestations that he was but a mere spectator caught up in the melee, poor Allan was sent home for the rest of the week and I don't think he ever forgave the youth who had quite unintentionally dumped him in the sand.

The weeks rolled by and slowly but surely the hidden mysteries of the Turner's trade were revealed to me, thanks in the main to David Beech's expert tutelage. During this period there had been a number of visits to the ambulance room for minor cuts and scrapes, which I learned very quickly were the Turner's unfortunate stock in trade. That and foreign bodies in the eye were our constant companions. Of course we learned to live with this collateral damage to our bodies and in any gathering of tradesmen it was always easy to identify the Turners. These were the guys with the scarred hands and missing or part missing digits. However, these industrial deformities were accepted as badges of honour and were always worth a drink at the bar when some inquisitive person asked, "How did that happen?" - And then out of the blue came the call.

Chapter 7 – First Placement

Once we fledgling tradesmen were considered reasonably competent enough to be let loose from the 'Pen' and into the various machine shops without, hopefully, not having lost an eye or too many fingers, we were assigned a factory and a department in which to ply our various trades. As a turner I, along with most of my fellow apprentices, were hoping that we would be sent to either the large and modern Spurrier Factory, were all the main engine components were made or perhaps even the older Farington Plant were many of the transmission parts were manufactured and assembled.

There was of course one other possibility and that was to be seconded to the dreaded North Works. Now North Works just happened to be the site of the original Leyland Motor's empire and little had changed there in the preceding 50 years or so. As I mentioned in an earlier chapter it was a rather gloomy and forbidding factory divided up into relatively small workshops, with conditions much like they were for the original workers. There was even a couple of sections where the machines were actually belt driven; the power coming from an overhead shaft that ran the length of that particular workshop.

However, what concerned us budding engineers most was the potential, or rather the lack of it, to earn big money. In those days, and well into the 70's, a large part of a shop floor worker's wage was made up by 'piecework' bonuses, which were added to a relatively lowly flat rate. For those of you who may be unfamiliar with the term 'piecework', it was a method of payment based on how many component parts or 'pieces' you produced in a given time.

This time was calculated by probably the most unpopular employees in the factory – the Time Study Engineers or Rate Fixers, as they were more commonly known. Now at the Spurrier Factory and the Farington Plant these guys were, as I mentioned, quite unpopular. However, at the North Works they were positively reviled. It appeared that old habits died hard in the North Works Time Study department as the piecework times allocated by the heartless incumbents were so low that there was hardly time left in the day for a toilet break (the terminology used for this bodily function was however a little more earthy as you would expect). This of course meant that earning high bonuses at the North Works was nigh on impossible compared with the opportunities at the other plants, where, as one fellow worker succinctly remarked, that although Rate Fixers there may have had hard hearts, at least it was better than the swinging brick, which was believed to be the inhuman organ possessed by the North Works crew.

With these facts in mind, the dozen or so apprentices to be assigned their postings that day sat and waited for 'Dad' (Harry Glassbrook) to inform us of our fate. Suffice it to say that as the Spurrier Factory and Farington Plant requirements were filled, much to the delight of those selected, Tom Holland, George Pails and myself were still awaiting our placements. With what appeared to be a rather malevolent gleam in his eye, 'Our Father' informed us that we were the 'lucky' ones as we were going to work in the original Leyland factory – Of course we all knew what that meant.

With heavy hearts we three made our way over to the North Works. Tom was assigned to 100 Department while George and I trudged further down the main passageway into 104 with instructions to report to the foreman – a certain Mr Albert Milner or 'Ebba' as he was more affectionately known. As was the custom in those days we were placed under the wing of a more practised machinist in order to experience first hand the ancient art of turning. After three or four days we were then permitted to 'have a go' unsupervised and I remember feeling very proud when I made, all by myself, my very first component part. I took to the art quite quickly and soon found myself working totally unsupervised. However, even at such tender years, we apprentices were expected to work at piecework rates to subsidise our miserly flat rates. Fortunately time allowances were made depending on your age and in my case with 50% extra time added to each component produced meant that I could earn myself a half decent bonus.

Now what should I do with all these bonus earnings? A dapper little gentleman called Jackie Bannister answered the burning question for me. Jackie was the workingman's answer to the high street bank. Every payday, he could be found doing the rounds of the factory with his moneybag and little notebook, collecting cash from his many customers who were generally putting aside a little money each week for such things as holidays and Christmas expenses. He persuaded me that I would never miss 'two bob' or 'half-a-crown' a week and how great it would be at holiday and Christmas time to be picking up an extra pound or two to spend.

On reflection I reckon I owe Jackie a huge vote of gratitude as thanks to his friendly persuasion he introduced me to the ethic of saving which continues to this day. It mattered little that he himself had probably the best holidays and most lavish Christmases thanks to the interest he earned from our meagre weekly contributions. However it mattered little, as it was a win-win situation for all concerned.

For any of you older readers who lived in the Leyland/Preston area, you may remember Jackie Bannister from the third hat that he wore. Not only was he an accomplished machinist and honest banker (yes – there is such a person), he was also a renowned ballroom dancer who could be found most evenings teaching the 'two left footers' of the region the genteel art of dancing at the Adriatic Ballroom in Preston that was run by a certain Wally Hobkirk – Happy days…

As was common with most manufacturing processes, Leyland Motors operated a multi-shift system. However, young apprentices were not expected to work on the nightshift until they had turned 18. Although a premium was paid for working the unsociable hours, there were not many 18 year-olds who readily volunteered for 'nights'. I remember well a certain foreman approaching me one day and enquiring how old I was.

"17," was my guarded response.

"When are you 18?" was his reply.

"Next Wednesday," I added.

"Right, you're on nights next Monday."

"But I'll still only be 17," I protested.

"Well I won't tell if you wont," he concluded with a grin. And so I had my first taste of shift work – an experience that I could have well lived without – but then again somebody had to do it.

There was however, one rather unexpected bonus for night shift workers who, after a hard night's graft had the good fortune to travel home to Preston by bus. My first experience of this journey caught me rather unawares. As I boarded the bus I noticed that most of my fellow passengers were making for the upper deck. Not only that, the majority were occupying the seats on one particular side of the bus. It was only as we passed a neat row of semi-detached houses in Tardy Gate that the reason for this unusual distribution of passengers became clear.

The curtains were thrown back and a light shone brightly from a bedroom window. All eyes were focused in the direction of that window – and there she sat; a young lady about to put on a very lacy and supportive item of clothing. The bus swayed ominously as all the upper deck passengers moved to the offside of the bus for a better view of the scene unfolding. A second or two later the window was passed despite frantic calls to the driver from one enthusiastic voyeur to 'slow down'. It transpired that this spectacle was a near daily occurrence and I believe the young lady in question enjoyed the attention almost as much as her many ardent male admirers. The wide smiles that ensued lasted all the way into Preston and I thought that if such an uplifting sight were available to the male working population every morning than productivity throughout the land would surely rise. I thought long and hard on this proposition only to discover that the Sun newspaper had beaten me to it – Oh how bitter the pangs of afterthought!

During these early years an event was to occur that I continue to practice up to this very day – I became a blood donor. I remember well that first time I was somewhat coerced into becoming a donor. I had just turned 18 when the blood donor nurses or 'Dracula's Dollies' as we had christened them, paid their bi-annual visit to the factory in search of 'victims'. I have to admit that at this particular time in my life I was not keen at all at the thought of giving blood and as the nurses came our way I dodged behind a large waste bin. Just when I thought the coast was clear, a voice whispered in my ear, "Have they gone?" "Yea, I think so," I replied, turning to see who had spoken to me. Imagine my horror to find it was one of the nurses, clipboard in hand waiting to take my details. Having being caught so embarrassingly, I hadn't the nerve to refuse – and she was such a pretty nurse as well. That first donation set the pattern for the next 60 years or so and I am proud to say that my continuing contributions to the blood bank, both in whole blood and more recently platelets, is now approaching the 200 mark.

I continued to serve the major part of my apprenticeship in the North Works and although I perhaps didn't appreciate it at the time the wide experience that I gained served me well for the promotions that were to follow. Not only did I master the craft of turning but due to the diversity of metal shaping machinery in the factory, I also became adept at milling, drilling and all forms of grinding.

Chapter 8 – Among The Elite

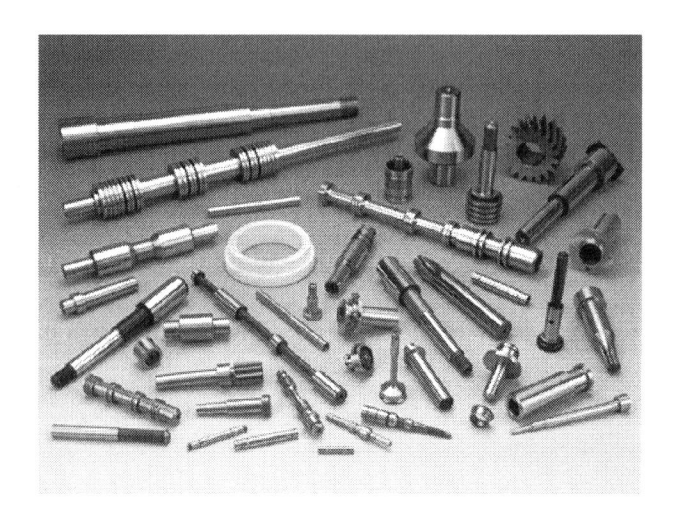

As I approached my final few months as an apprentice, I realized that although now being reasonably proficient in most forms of metal shaping, there were aspects of the trade that I had not yet mastered. I therefore requested a move to the Tool Room, which was situated at the Farington Plant. There I would hopefully complete my training by mastering such techniques as screw cutting and jig boring. However, there was a further motive in requesting a move to the Tool Room as I reasoned that with a bit of luck I might just be retained there when I turned 21. The appeal of such a final placement was that not only would I be working among an elite class of tradesmen but I would also be free of the dreaded piecework as this was not a factor that affected the wage packets of the privileged Tool Room operatives.

As I walked through the doors of the Tool Room, the sight of a huge WW2 bomb greeted me. It appeared that sometime during the war years this particular bomb had fallen on the building but thankfully had failed to explode. (It is interesting to note that the bomb did not disappear when the site was eventually closed and can now be seen in the Museum of Lancashire in Preston). Standing next to the bomb, in earnest conversation with a foreman, was the Tool Room superintendent, a certain Mr Tommy Halton. He noticed my hesitancy and quickly put me at ease by introducing himself and the foreman before proceeding to give me a guided tour of his domain; a kindness that I never forgot during my stay in the Tool Room and in my future dealings with him.

I did indeed complete my knowledge of all aspects of metal shaping in the few months that I spent in the Tool Room, despite being reminded that I was not on piecework now and to limit my output to match that of my fellow toolmakers. I was just beginning to think that I could get used to this new more leisurely life when just before my 21st birthday I was summoned to Tom Halton's office. He thanked me for my efforts and informed me that he had been keen to keep me under his wing. However, it transpired that my old boss in 104 was also eager to have me back and had sweetened the request by adding that he had plans for me which would further my career. It was with some reluctance that I bade farewell to the many friends I had made in the Tool Room and once again I picked up my trusty toolbox and made my way back to the North Works.

A little addendum to the time I spent in the Tool Room was to learn that Mr Halton had put my name forward as a contender for the prestigious 'Apprentice of the Year' award. No fairytale ending unfortunately, as although I didn't win it, as a nominee I was presented with a set of micrometers by no less a personage than Sir William

Lyons, the co-founder of Jaguar cars. However, as I mentioned in an earlier Chapter, my life as a turner at Leyland Motors was about to be interrupted – or was it?

Chapter 9 – National Service – Or Not?

By now I was courting strongly with Margaret and in 1958, the year I finally became a fully-fledged tradesman and also gained my National certificate, we became engaged. It was somewhat unfortunate for all concerned that as I approached my majority, there was another rather important lady vying for my attention – and this lady you ignored at your peril. She was very sweet, wore a crown and positively insisted that I became a member of her institution – the Armed Forces that is! Yes, in 1958 National Service was still a must for all able-bodied young men and despite being granted a dispensation to complete my apprenticeship, the fateful day eventually dawned when mum met me at the front door holding a very official looking buff envelope. It was, as I had anticipated, a letter from the rather important lady's representative, 'inviting' me to attend the local drill hall the following week in order to establish as to which branch of HM's forces I was best suited for.

The day went well as did the medical and subsequent interview and despite being rejected by the RAF, I was reasonably happy to be informed that due to my engineering background, I was to join the Royal Armoured Corp and providing the results from my medical were satisfactory I would be receiving a letter within the next few days, which would include a travel warrant to Bovington Camp in Dorset where I would be undergoing my initial training. By now my previous despondency at the thoughts of two years in the forces was fading. In fact I was quite looking forward to the challenge that it presented. Even 'She who was to be left behind' had just about come to terms with the prospect of an enforced parting and had promised to write to me every day – and so I waited for the official promised letter.

On the day that the expected letter arrived, it was accompanied by another equally official looking document, both bearing the same OHMS crest. Dad laughed and joked that it looked like I was getting two postings. Sure enough the first letter confirmed my expected arrival at Bovington on a specified date – unfortunately the second was something of a bombshell. *Dear Sir,* it began, *we are writing to inform you that as a result of your recent medical you have been placed in Grade 4 and are therefore considered unfit for military service. Details have been forwarded to your own GP and we suggest you contact the surgery at your earliest convenience.* You could have knocked me down with a feather. I feared the worse! There was not an ailment or disease in the medical dictionary that I did not imagine I had contracted.

The strange thing was I felt absolutely fine. Nevertheless an appointment was made and off I went to see Dr Howard, my GP in his West Cliff surgery in Preston.

Now Dr Howard was an ex-military man and as I entered his consulting room I was greeted not with any enthusiasm or sympathy but with a rather hostile and contemptuous stare.

"How on earth did you manage to swing this?" was his opening remark to me.

"Swing what?" I replied somewhat bemused.

"Getting yourself classified as unfit for military service." I assured him that all I had done was present my body for inspection without a word being spoken (although I do recall a little cough whilst being handled rather unceremoniously!), the decision to assess me as being unfit was entirely out of my hands. The good doctor was not entirely convinced but at least proceeded to inform me as to the reason why I had been placed in such a low category.

"You have one kidney slightly larger than the other," he told me indignantly.

"Is that serious?" I enquired anxiously.

"If it is then about half of the people in the country are afflicted with the 'problem'" he added. "No! It's not at all serious; in fact it is very common. Why the medical board have used this reason to place you in grade 4 is beyond me. However, if you like I can write to them and say that in my opinion you are totally fit for service."

I thought long and hard on his suggestion and a full two seconds had elapsed before I thanked him for his concern but in this situation and being a firm believer in 'kismet' I thought it circumspect to accept the board's decision. I hurried from the surgery followed by a volley of muffled expletives from a man who was now more convinced than ever that I had been 'swinging the lead'.

Needless to say the whole family were delighted when I broke the news to them that I was not suffering from some terrible ailment although I must confess that part of me was a little sad that I would not be serving in HM forces. However, I consoled myself with the fact that as a time served tradesman I would now be earning about five times the amount I would have done if I had been conscripted. My short sojourn in the tool room also came to an end that eventful week and so I resumed my trade as a turner back in the good old 104 department at North Works.

Chapter 10 – Return to 104

My continuance as a civilian now confirmed, I returned to the 104 machine shop a few days before my 21st birthday to find that many of the ancient lathes, which rumour suggested had been 'second hand' when they had been used to fashion spearheads for Caesar's troops, had been replaced. In the 1950's these new machines called preoptive lathes were the last word in turning technology and I was surprised but gratified when our foreman, Albert Milner, informed me that I was to operate one. It was like upgrading from a Model T Ford to a Rolls Royce - Gosh! What a difference they made to earning capabilities, well at least up to the time before our redoubtable Time Study manager realized that piecework earnings were increasing to unprecedented levels and sent in his ever popular engineers to reassess the original time allowances – still it was profitable while it lasted.

I became quite adept at operating this new generation of machinery and within the year I received my first promotion and escaped the clutches of the dreaded piecework system forever – I was made a Machine Tool Setter. This duty entailed tooling or setting up the various machines for the operators as they moved from the manufacture of one component part to another. This gave me the opportunity to explore different and more cost effective ways of producing parts and helped supplement my wage packet through awards for these improvements via the Suggestion Scheme that was in operation. As I was to be married to Margaret the following year, this extra cash allowed us to reach our mortgage deposit target much quicker than we had initially anticipated…

Life was good. I was happy at my work. Margaret and I had tied the knot early in 1960. We had moved into a brand new semi-detached house in Tardy Gate that cost us all of £1,795 and tied us into a mortgage of £3-6s-8d per month. It was just a year later; soon after Janet our first-born had arrived when tragedy struck. Each morning would find me waiting for the bus on the main Preston to Leyland road. However, it was not very often that I actually caught the bus. Quite a number of my workmates had motorbikes or scooters and would more often than not stop and give me a free ride into work on the back of their bikes.

In particular there were three guys who would regularly stop. Ken and Dave both had high-powered machines and the pair drove as if they were attempting to break the land speed record. It was not unusual, if the conditions allowed, for them to hit the 'ton' when going down the Bashall straight. Tom on the other hand, a far more sober young man who plodded sedately along on his scooter, was the one I preferred to ride with as I didn't really appreciate too many adrenalin rushes or skid marks in unmentionable places at 7 o'clock in the morning.

It was somewhat ironic then when on one particular morning whilst travelling to work at a sensible speed on the back of Tom's scooter that the accident occurred. We were on the final lap in School Lane in Leyland when the scooter hit a pile of loose chippings. Tom could do nothing to avert what happened next. He unfortunately lost control as the scooter was spun round sending me flying – that is until I hit the concrete lamp standard with an almighty thump.

The next thing I remember was waking up in Chorley Hospital with the mother and father of all headaches and extreme gravel rash on my legs and torso – but at least I was still in one piece. I was lying in a snug hospital bed, my head wound had been stitched very neatly and the junior doctor who was taking my pulse, in a laconic attempt at hospital humour he informed me that I had been very fortunate that only my head had come into contact with the post as it was obviously the most resilient part of my anatomy. I was discharged the following day and fortunately there were no lasting consequences – apart from the 2-inch scar in the hairline of my scalp, which I carry to this day.

Chapter 11 – Machine Shop Shenanigans

Of all the plants, departments, shops and offices that I worked in during my time at Leyland Motors, I don't think there was one that contained as many 'characters' as the ones I came across in the 104 Machine shop. These men were among the poorest paid but I don't think there was a happier and more carefree bunch of guys in the whole of the Leyland group. They worked hard for their relatively scant rewards but by golly they knew how to have fun as well. Despite having to beat the clock to make a half-decent wage, there always appeared to be time for a joke or a leg-pull. I could probably fill a book with all the lively action but will content myself with sharing with you just some of the more memorable stunts.

Tommy B was probably the principal joker in the pack, always looking for ways to get his fellow workmates 'going', in the nicest possible way of course. One of his favourite tricks was to sneak up behind one of his colleagues and paint the heels of their boots or shoes with white paint. I don't think there was a man in the whole of the machine shop that had escaped Tommy's dubious artwork on their heels – apart from one that is. Bob Whittaker was the shop's sample inspector and prided himself on his vigilance and ability to escape the dreaded brush – or so he thought. Now Bob may have been vigilant but Tommy was extremely resolute and determined. One morning Bob was standing at his sample table with one eye on the component part he was checking and the other for any sign of our would-be artist. Little did he realize that the dogged Tommy was crawling underneath Bob's locker, loaded paintbrush in hand and about to do the dirty? He almost made it as well until he inadvertently broke wind due to his cramped position. The sound was enough to alert Bob and in readiness for such an attack he reached into his drawer, removed an egg and smashed it over poor Tommy's head. Even at this undignified conclusion to his low level approach he emerged grinning with the remains of the egg running down his face. We spectators, knowing Tommy only to well, figured that this would not be the end of the affair.

The buzzer sounded the start of the afternoon stint and Bob stood at his table with the self-satisfied look on his face that proclaimed to all 'that nobody gets the better of me'. His first customer of the day laid down his sample and casually remarked, "Why are your heels white Bob?" Bob visibly paled as he glanced down to find that not only the heels but also the sides of his work shoes were indeed brilliant white. The fusillade of oaths that followed is unfortunately unprintable. It transpired that during the lunch break, Bob had visited the local Post Office, oblivious to the fact that he was being followed by you-know-who. His guard well and truly down, Bob had transacted his business, sublimely unaware that his shoes were being transformed into 'a whiter shade of pale'. To make matters worse when he had partially recovered from the grim discovery, he found stuck on his locker a notice that announced in block capitals 'HA-HA-HA! THE YOLKS ON YOU NOW'. Despite the immediate angry reaction, Bob was man enough to realize the funny side of the escapade and the shift ended with handshakes and backslaps all round. Mind you it was a few weeks before Tommy got his samples passed as easily as he had before his 'brush' with Bob.

Another old Lancashire tradition that I believe originated in the county's textile mills, but was certainly well supported in the North Works, was the 'Chamber Pot Climb.' The ritual was performed on newly married men when they were given a gaudily decorated chamber pot, usually with a large eye painted on the bottom. This does not mean it was merely presented to them; in fact they had to work jolly hard for the dubious honour of possessing it. The chamber pot would be securely fastened high up in the roof beams of the workshop. The 'victim' then had to scale a ladder to reach it, free it from its fastenings and bring it down intact. This act was accomplished to the accompaniment of virtually every worker in the factory hammering on any suitable metallic surface within striking distance. The noise was ear shattering and had to be heard to be believed. It was certainly great fun to watch but when it became my turn to undergo the ordeal it was rather a different story.

I had seen the somewhat pathetic attempts to free the 'jerry' by those who had gone before me and was determined to scale the ladder better prepared. About my person I had an assortment of spanners and other tools that I believed would simplify the task of freeing the pot but unfortunately my so-called mates were one step ahead of me. They had secured the infamous 'potty' with a length of stout chain, the end links padlocked securely together.

As I scaled the ladder the cacophony of noise began, the rafters above me shook ominously at the din created and my knees shook when I eventually reached my 'prize'. A minute later I was climbing back down with the unbroken trophy clutched firmly in my hand. 'How on earth did you manage that' you may ask? Well until today it has remained a closely guarded secret, which to you, dear reader, I shall now reveal.

The padlock had come with a spare key and a few minutes before I began my ascent I was taken aside by a 'friend' who offered me the spare key in exchange for 'two bob' (10p) coupled with the promise to keep my mouth shut. Suffice it to say I was more than happy to accept the dual deal as otherwise I reckon I might have been up that ladder yet trying to free that blasted chamber pot.

Another outstanding memory was the time when the whole of North Works decided to collect silver paper to assist in the purchase of guide dogs for the blind. This very laudable activity was conducted by each man adding his contribution to the ever increasing silver paper ball and passing it to other workmates, who added their personal contribution in a similar fashion. The resulting silver paper sphere was then passed onto the next department for the guys there to add their contribution to the ever-increasing globe. The idea really caught on and soon these increasingly growing silver balls were passing through each department on a daily basis. After a couple of weeks or so, someone inquired as to where all these precious balls were being stored as surely there was now enough silver paper to buy a whole pack of guide dogs.

"I think it's Scouse Fred in 100 shop that's storing 'em," said our Tommy from 104. "I pass the balls onto him after we've done our bit,"

"No! He passes them on to Big Jim in 102," responded Black Bob. "I guess he must be storing them somewhere."

"Nay he passes 'em to Tiny in 105," said Burscough Bob. "I've seen him do it." Now this conversation went on for some time before the penny finally dropped. It transpired that no one was actually storing the balls; in fact it turned out that there were no great stock of silver paper balls as such apart from the one that was going round in one big circle.

When this revelation became common knowledge (and it took all of 20 minutes to reach every corner of the factory) it initially caused a sense of initial disappointment. However, true to their type, all the men (and many ladies to) realized that the task was not going to be as easy as it first appeared; so did this little setback deter them from the task? Not on your Nelly. I believe it made everybody involved more determined than ever to reach the target set. With renewed vigour the silver paper chase began again and despite heroic efforts from all concerned, it took many months of determined collecting before the objective was finally achieved. The silver paper was duly delivered to the organization that was running the campaign and the illuminated certificate that was received, thanking all for their efforts, took pride of place in the North Work's Superintendent's office for many years.

In the telling of this little story, you will have noted the reference to people with names such as 'Black Bob', 'Tiny', 'Big Jim' and Burscough Bob. This giving of nicknames was quite a common occurrence in the Leyland factories then, as no doubt it is now, and usually reflected a characteristic such as where they were from, a physical appearance or some other attribute unique to the individual. North Works was right up there with this trend and it was a rare individual that did not possess an alias that he or she was better known by – well at work anyway. Names that spring to mind include 'Boss Brooks', 'Buckets', 'Buttercup', 'Ebba' and his brother 'Rush', 'Spot On', 'Airwick' and Sweaty Betty (you wouldn't want to stand to close to either of those two), Harry Fiver,' 'Skenny Joe,' 'Ding-Dong and of course we had our share of 'Chalky Whites,' 'Nobby Clarks,' 'Dusty Millers and ' Bomber Harris's', plus a whole litany of those unutterable monikers that would definitely be considered to be either racist, sexually inappropriate or just to politically incorrect to print in this day and age. However they were all used and accepted in the right spirit and even today it never fails to bring a fond smile to my face when I recall the lads and lasses who were affectionately re-christened - Leyland Motors style.

Chapter 12 – Time For a Break – The Ball

Mind you, it was not all work and no play at T'motors. As well as the various indoor pastimes and outdoor sports facilities that were available for employees, there was also the famous once a year treat of the LEYLAND MOTORS BALL that was generally held on a Friday evening in March at the famous WINTER GARDENS in Blackpool. The planning for this ever-popular annual event was conducted with near military precision. Coaches were hired to convey the many hundreds of employees and their partners from all corners of Lancashire and timed to arrive at the Winter Gardens at predetermined intervals in order to avoid congestion - and it worked well.

The venue offered something for everyone, depending of course on your age, sex and relationship status. You could probably group the attendees into two categories, those with marital partners or sweethearts and those of both sexes who were young, footloose and fancy-free. Over the many years of attending I can claim to have been a paid-up member of both camps and whilst the former group attended mainly for the dancing and socializing with friends, the latter set, particularly the males of the species had two principle aims. The first was to have a good drinking session in one of the many bars, the second to survey the 'talent' with a view perhaps to 'copping off' for the night.

As a young apprentice, just old enough to drink legally (well near enough), my first couple of visits with the 'lads' comprised initially of the mandatory 'supping session' at the busiest bar, the oldest looking youth delegated to place the order while the rest of the gang kept a weather eye open for any unattached females who had the audacity to stray into what then was a virtual male preserve. Suitably refreshed we would then wend (stagger) our way to the dance floor and peruse the 'talent'. If you were lucky you might just catch the eyes of two young ladies dancing together and a quick consultation with your buddy would determine who was going to dance with whom. Many of these tacit approaches were met with rebuff but just occasionally you struck lucky and received the nod of perhaps resigned acceptance, depending on the lateness of the hour and the level of desperation reached by both parties. Now depending on your boldness, perhaps fuelled by a couple of OBJ's and after the usual obligatory and inane queries such as 'Do you come here often?' or 'Where are you from?' and depending on your chosen one's reaction you might perhaps then enquire, 'Would you like to go for a drink after?' More often than I care to remember, this final supplication was answered with, 'Can't – I'm with me mates,' or 'Don't you think you've had enough?' or on one very memorable occasion being informed that her boyfriend wouldn't approve – he's looking daggers at me now!' However, and depending on your tenacity, you were sometimes given the nod of assent.

As the music died you would then escort your newfound friend to one of the more salubrious drinking establishments such as the cosy Galleon Bar. A couple of 'Snowballs' or 'Babychams' later you might suggest a stroll to the balcony, there to gaze victoriously at the madding crowd below, including perhaps some of your less fortunate buddies still seeking a similar prize to that you were now surreptitiously slipping your arm around. This manoeuvre successfully achieved you would perhaps risk a peck on the cheek, which with a bit of luck might even turn into a full-blown 'snog', only to be rudely interrupted by a tap on the shoulder from one of the ever vigilant stewards, followed by a stern reminder that 'There's none of that there allowed 'ere.' Depending on the depth of attraction you would then perhaps ask her which coach she had come on in the hopes that it would be somewhere close to your home and that a furtherance of your amorous activity could be continued on the back seat. I was never that fortunate. The one and only time I 'pulled' to such a degree was with a young lady from Wigan and as gorgeous as she was, a 15 mile walk back to Preston in the wee small hours was, I considered, hardly fair compensation for a non-guaranteed romantic interlude.

The next working day would be spent doing the rounds of your mates, enquiring as to how they had fared on the night. Now boys being boys, if one was to believe all the late-night shenanigans that had taken place under the pier that particular evening then there would have been no room for the tide to come in! – Ah! Happy days.

Sharing a drink with friends in the Galleon Lounge

Chapter 13 – More Breaks - Sports Day

The first Saturday in July was a very special day in the hearts of many Leyland people, citizens and employees alike, especially those with sporty or competitive aspirations. For as long as any one could remember, all thoughts of work were set firmly aside on this special date as this was Sports Day and whether you were participating or just going along as a spectator, it was definitely an event not to be missed. Those sporting enthusiasts with long memories of the occasion swore blind that they had never known it to rain on Sports Day and from my own personal experiences I have to admit that despite the odd damp morning, come 1 o'clock you could guarantee that the sun would break through on the proceedings.

So what was it that made Leyland Motors Sports Day such a special event? I dare say you would hear many different reasons depending on whom you asked. Which regular attendee could ever forget the unusual but extremely effective gait of George Lamb as year after year he won the senior walking event. Even when they introduced a handicap system, George always managed to literally 'walk' away with the winner's medal. It was said by one cynic that if they made him walk backwards, blindfolded, carrying two buckets of sand he would still probably cross the line first. For me however, it was the diversity of the events and participants that made sports day so memorable. If you were serious about your sport then all the usual activities were there to enter. For those with more modest athletic ambitions and perhaps with a lighter heart, one could also enter the less solemn proceedings such as the greasy pole contest; the tug of war affair or even the 3-legged race. These were all fun events, which I believe the majority of spectators enjoyed the most.

However, as a callow youth of 17 summers, my overriding ambition on that particular sports day in 1954 was to partake in the General Manager's Cup, not with any hope of winning it I might add but just for the thrill of taking part. This coupled with the arm-twisting from our fiery Welsh college tutor, Viv Yeo, who doubled as a PT instructor and whose Celtic philosophy included the firm belief that non-participants in all forms of sport were 'nowt' but a load of cissies. Now the GM's Cup was a competition for apprentices of 18 years and under and consisted (if memory serves me right) of six events; the 100, 220, 440 and 880 yard races, plus the long and the high jump. The scoring system was akin to the modern day pentathlon event and the youth with highest number of accumulated points was declared the winner and held the cup for the next 12 months. It was a handicapped event in order to encourage lads of various ages and abilities to take part.

Now it is at this point that I must declare that I was never renowned for my running prowess. I guess that flat out I could probably run as fast as George Lamb could walk, and even that's debateable. My best chances of getting any points on the board was therefore in the 2 jump events. I say this because the young lady I was stepping out with at the time was quite sporty and her long legs made her a natural at both the high and the long jumps. We often used to visit Penwortham Holme a multi sports venue that served the active people of South Preston and surrounding area. There we would have a go at most of the events on offer, which included of course both jumping disciplines. I quite surprised myself when with a little encouragement from the long-legged one, I found myself clearing the high jump bar at the 5ft mark and leaving footprints in the sand at about 17ft from the take-off point. Neither figure was likely to set any records but at least I had the satisfaction of (almost) beating my girlfriend.

These rather secretive training sessions were of course unknown to my potential opponents but more importantly to Mr Yeo, the chief handicapper, who gleaned his knowledge of a contestant's abilities from their performances in the college gym'. This handicapping was conducted in the presence of those taking part in order to give each one the opportunity to discuss his handicap – I can see the scene now! "Rogerson, you run like a big girl and probably jump like one to." I looked suitably offended but said nothing. "I'm going to give you 6-inches for the high and a foot for the long jump." I remained impassive. Similar generous amounts were given me for the track events, which I knew would still not get me a podium place, but I was more than happy with the starts given for the field events.

I can imagine now what you are all thinking. This is going to be a fairytale ending as I walk off into the sunset carrying the prestigious GM cup. Well unfortunately it didn't quite happen like that. Oh! I won the high jump of course, thanks to the generous handicap from an irate Welshman who never quite forgave me for 'conning' him. If he'd given me another 2-inches in the long jump I'd have won that one as well. However, Geoff Hough, the eventual cup winner, managed to beat me by the narrowest of margins. I finished 4th overall and was well pleased with the outcome and I guess that this small measure of success endeared me to Leyland Sports Day right up to the sad time when for various reasons, it came to an end. They were happy times and friendships were formed at the event that has lasted to this very day…

The young lady I mentioned earlier also introduced me to the great game of tennis, a pastime I enjoy active involvement in up to this very day. After my rather fortuitous performance at the Leyland Sports Day and realizing that any sporting prowess that I might aspire to was never likely to be in either track or field events, I was delighted to learn in later years that the Sports Day activities included a doubles tennis tournament. This involved the names of all entrants being placed in a hat and drawn out in pairs. Each duo would play a short set against all the other partnerships and whichever pairing won the most sets would be declared the winners. Again this was not destined to my 'Andy Murray' moment although with the partner I had drawn, a certain well-established tennis player by the name of Harold Moss, we finished in a fairly respectable position. Little did I know then that this fortuitous partnership would lead me to a lifetime of playing the really beautiful game?

As we rounded off the day like all dedicated tennis aficionados with tea and cucumber sandwiches, Harold asked me if I was a member of any of the local tennis clubs. I told him that I had considered it but as yet had taken it no further. "Why not join us at our club?" he suggested. "I reckon you have the making of a decent club player." Ego suitably massaged I told him that I would certainly consider it. However, other priorities were taking precedence during that particular time of my life and it was to be many years later before Margaret and I eventually joined the Leyland Tennis Club.

As we walked onto the courts on that first evening I was met with a cheery shout from the clubhouse. "You took your time didn't you?" It was the aforesaid Harold Moss. A little older, carrying a little more weight and sporting a little less hair, yet despite his advancing years, still a tennis force to be reckoned with. We played together for many years and most of the few tennis skills that I acquired were without doubt thanks to the coaching and encouragement from Harold – A true gentleman. It was a sad day for the community in general and tennis in particular when Harold passed away. He was and still is sadly missed by his many friends in the tennis world.

During my time at the club I played in most of the teams including a purple patch in the late 1970's and early 80's, when the 1st team won the local Ribble Tennis League in four consecutive years. As the years advanced, younger and better players took my place in the top team, which of course is how it should be in all sports, yet my passion for the game never waned and I was as happy playing for the 4th's as I had been when wielding my racket and picking up trophies in the 1st team – Happy days!

Ribble League Division 1 Winners – 1978

Willie Cunningham presents the trophies - 1979

Winners again - 1980

And again - 1981

Chapter 14 – A Seaside Break

The caring side of the company manifested itself in many ways, particularly with their attitude towards the younger employees. In the 1950's holidays abroad were practically unheard of and even breaks in the country or at the seaside in those more austere days were not the inalienable right of many working class families, as they appear to be today. Recognising this, the company organized a summer break for their lesser-privileged 17/18 year-old apprentices to coincide with the annual shutdown of the factory.

Those of us who were fortunate enough to be selected for the hallowed break would gather at the South Works gates on the appointed day, clutching battered suitcases, and waiting somewhat impatiently for the bus that would ferry us to our intended holiday destination – Kessingland Youth Camp in sunny Suffolk. The site had previously been a WW2 army camp and comprised of wooden huts set out in military camp fashion. Most of the huts were dormitories with bunk style sleeping arrangements. On arrival we soon realized that the camp was huge and accommodated young people of both sexes and was truly international. As well as us 'Brits' we discovered we were sharing our camp with Dutch, Italian, Belgium and best of all – the French.

Now you may be pondering as to why I should be enthusing so passionately over our near neighbours across the channel. Well, the keyword here has to be 'passionately'. You must bear in mind that we were not yet in the 'swingin sixties' where, to quote the old song, 'Anything Goes'. The mid-fifties were more like the line from the same song that suggested that a 'glimpse of stocking was simply shocking' – Well this was certainly true of a bunch of wide-eyed, innocent and naïve 17-year-olds from Lancashire who had luckily met up with their more free-spirited and less conventional neighbours from across the channel that particular summer…

Where should I begin? Perhaps that particular balmy evening when replete from a plain but wholesome dinner and accompanied by a couple of pals, we strolled along the near deserted sand and pebble beach. As we approached a more secluded cove we heard voices that were undoubtedly feminine and most definitely foreign. We clambered over a series of boulders to discover that the owners of the voices were indeed of the fairer sex who were enjoying a spot of late sunbathing. All very conventional you might think; nothing to get excited about. Well that would have been true apart from the fact that at least half of the young ladies were topless and appeared quite unabashed by our sudden and unannounced presence!
"Bon Jour," was the united cry from the girls accompanied by friendly waves as though this was an ordinary everyday experience for them.

"Hiya," came the somewhat strangled response from three very dry and nervous throats and not really sure where they should be directing their eyes.

"Why not come and join us? – We've got beer!"

Was this really Kessingland, or had we just died and gone to heaven? A balmy eve', a gentle breeze, topless girls – and BEER! As another old song goes, 'who could ask for anything more!' Suffice it to say that the rest of the evening passed all to quickly and as the sun dipped towards the horizon and shadows lengthened, all sense of time was lost. Not surprisingly as the beer flowed and friendships were established, time was not the only thing 'lost' that night but propriety forbids me to add further detail. Suffice it to say that much later that night, three slightly inebriated youths staggered back into camp wearing the cheesiest grins you are ever likely to see.

It was only right and proper that having been introduced to the delights of 'l'amour' - Gallic style that we repay our fellow campers by teaching them something that we 'Brits' were reasonably proficient at during the fifties – Football. And so a match was duly arranged with a morning kick-off. Now I'm not suggesting for a minute that the French are devious bas****s or that their invitation to party in their quarters the evening before the match was anything but 'mains sur la mer' or perhaps even l'esprit de parti (see we did learn something) but climbing back into our bunks just as dawn was breaking did not bode well for a 10-30am kick-off.

A dozen or so bleary-eyed youths emerged from their huts just before the appointed hour. They wore an odd collection of crumpled shorts, creased shirts and footwear ranging from sandals to plimsolls (the forerunner of trainers) and not a football boot between the lot of them. The sight that met them hardly added confidence to their apparent collective hangover. A similar number of immaculately turned out 'Frenchies' were engaged in a variety of warm up exercises, cheered on by their own enthusiastic female fan club, who all appeared to be wearing very short shorts and tops that appeared to be at least two sizes to small. We contented ourselves with a kick-in until the hastily appointed and somewhat reluctant Italian referee blew his whistle and called us to order.

The French team kicked off, were quickly dispossessed by a typically weighty English tackle from Dave our burly centre forward, who spying the French goalie chatting up a particularly tight shirted female fan, whacked the ball goal wards and was delighted to see it sail just under the bar with the 'keeper not even aware that the game had commenced. One nil up and we'd hardly broken sweat. That inspiring start set the pattern for the rest of the game and despite their immaculate dress code and the impressive pre-match work out, one thing was for certain – they couldn't play football. It was after we had reached double figures without any response from our opponents that a member of their supervisory minders hauled half the team off and sent on about twice the number of the scantily dressed girls as substitutes.

The game that ensued could hardly be called football but there was no doubt that who ever had dubbed it a contact sport was certainly correct with the antics that followed – and they even managed to score a goal, much to the mortification of the guys who had been replaced. However, it all ended very amicably with cries of 'Viva La François' and 'Rule Britannia' ringing out across the camp and I think more was achieved by the young people of both countries that day in cementing Anglo – French relations than any other political assembly before or since. It was with heavy hearts (and a few broken ones as well) when a few short days later, both parties had to pack up and return to their respective homes. From that sublime week in deepest Suffolk I have always thought of France and its people with joy in my heart – that is until the time when I had to work with them! Ah! But that's a story for a much later chapter.

Chapter 15 – Shop Trips & Cabarets

100 Shop Trip – Circa 1960

By now I'm sure you are getting the picture that despite working long and hard for a living at Leyland Motors, there always seemed to be time for socializing with ones workmates. However, as well as the 'Ball' and 'Sports Days' in which to enjoy yourself with friends, it would be unforgivable of me to skip over the annual departmental trips and cabarets that were enjoyed by so many.

Regardless of which shop or department you worked in, the trips had a more or less common theme. They were usually planned for the summer months and a coach would be hired to convey the eager 'trippers' to either a pub with a bowling green; a pub with a dartboard or snooker table or a racecourse or greyhound stadium with a pub adjacent (have you spotted the common theme yet – No? – well carry on reading.

The coach would pull in at the chosen pub and after suitable liquid refreshment had been consumed then the sporting activities would commence. If the day were fine then it would be a knockout competition on the bowling green. If the weather were inclement then a darts, cards or snooker contest would ensue, all these activities would be undertaken to the accompaniment of pint glasses clinking and the rattle of plates as the sandwiches were passed around. By late afternoon it mattered little who had won the games, as now it was time to move on for the evening's entertainment. This would usually be in a social or working men's' club where food, entertainment and of course beer was available.

At the end of a most enjoyable day, the trippers would again return to the coach to be transported home. I can never ever remember departing on time. There was always at least a couple of guys missing, although a search of the toilets usually proved fruitful as it was there more often than not where the miscreants were to be found and assisted back to the coach.

When the coach finally did get underway you would imagine that the day was over – but you would be wrong as it was now that massed vocal chords, suitably lubricated, came into their own. However, as well as the community murdering of well loved songs, there was also solo performances and whoever can forget the dulcet tones of 'Two Songs Bob' whose renditions of Jim Reeves classics would have brought tears to a glass eye.

The most memorable trip that I went on was in 1964. I had just been informed that I was to be made a foreman and I was soon to become a father for the second time and Preston North End were in the semi-final of the FA Cup - and my cup literally runneth over. A trip was arranged to Villa Park to watch the match and a social club was booked in the Birmingham area to either celebrate or drown our sorrows after the game. The weather turned out to be foul on the day of the match in March and our merry band of trippers found themselves on the open terraces, totally exposed to the torrential rain that ensued for the duration of the match.

Swansea score first – But those smiles soon turned to tears

However, despite going a goal down in the first half, the PNE boys came out for the second half a totally transformed team. Alex (The Black Prince) Dawson equalised from the penalty spot and Tony Singleton smashed the winner from fully 30yards out and despite the rain running from us, all feelings of discomfort were banished. As we made our way back to the coach I shall never forget the sight of 'Moff' a dyed in the wool supporter, who I believe on that momentous day inadvertently introduced face painting to the soccer scene. He had a huge PNE rosette pinned to his cap and after two hours or so in the driving rain the colours had run from his favour forming symmetrical blue and white stripes down his face. Did he care? Not a jot and his entrance into the social club later that day drew thunderous cheers from the neutral 'Brummies'. On reflection I should have patented this idea of painting club colours on the face. I could have made a fortune – Ah me, once again the cruel pangs of afterthoughts raise their mocking head…

With such a famous win behind us there was no doubt that a further trip would be arranged to see our team perform under the twin towers of Wembley stadium. Well of course it was – Unfortunately I had to give up my precious ticket and place on the coach. As I mentioned earlier, I was about to become a father for the second time and with rather unfortunate timing, younger daughter Ruth arrived just five days before the staging of the final. I thought of every possible excuse under the sun to forego my paternal duties for just that one day but in the end I realized it would be churlish to allow three-year old Janet to wander the streets in my absence, even if it was only for the one day (Only kidding Janet – Honest!). After watching the game on TV I was rather glad I had not made the long trip to Wembley. PNE were beaten in the cruellest fashion, as despite holding the lead twice they finally succumbed to a 90th minute goal and I believe the homeward trip would have been painful and utterly demoralising.

If the trips were male dominated, then the cabarets gave the opportunity for workmates to bring along their wives and sweethearts (but not both to the same function). Many firm friendships were made at the cabarets and many are still thriving to this day. It was an opportunity for the younger guys to bring along and show off their latest girl and the married ones to leave the ladies to the latest gossip while they retired to the upstairs lounge for a swift 'half' or two.

The cabarets were hugely popular and the LMSAC ballroom was in constant demand for the staging of these functions. During the cabaret season, virtually every department, shop or office within the company held at least one such function during the year. The cabarets tended to follow a set pattern. There would be a period for meeting and greeting friends and generally socializing. This would be followed by a dance or two with live music provided by a local trio or quartet. Then there would be a break for buffet style refreshments and the action would recommence with either songs from a vocalist or jokes from a comedian. The concluding hour or so would once again be spent on the dance floor until time would finally be called when the musicians signed off by playing of 'The Last Waltz'.

Now these cabarets had all to be arranged beforehand with such requirements as the hiring of the band and entertainment and arrangements for the catering. Over the years, one man became quite famous for taking on these duties and often acting as compare for the event as well. That man was Bert Kenyon, who I had the pleasure of working alongside for more years than I suppose either of us care to remember. Because of his dedication in ensuring that everything went smoothly, he was more popularly known at Leyland Motors as 'Mr Cabaret'. It may be a bit late in the day but I would like to thank you Bert for the hard work and dedication that you provided in staging the cabarets that were so enjoyable to Margaret and me and I'm sure to many hundreds of ex-employees as well.

Chapter 16 – Climbing Up the Ladder

I did not know it at the time but my relatively short period as a machine tool setter was destined to come to an end. As I punched my clock card on that particular morning in early March 1964, Phil Gates, the senior foreman of 104, beckoned me into his office. There he informed me that later that morning I was to be interviewed by no less a personage than Les Southworth, the General Manager. It appeared that a vacancy for a foreman was soon to arise in the machine shop due to the elevation to a more senior position of the current incumbent and that I had been mentioned as a possible replacement.

Now Les Southworth was, to many of the people who were privileged to work with him, just slightly under the ranking order of God. You can therefore imagine how I felt when later that day I stood outside his office, heart beating madly, palms sweating profusely, waiting for the call to enter the hallowed ground. I managed to talk myself into the probable position of an 'also ran'. Surely there were more deserving and better-qualified candidates than me for the job? By the time I entered the inner sanctum I was totally calm. I convinced myself that I had nothing to lose as I could not possibly be selected for the position and would therefore treat the interview as a practice run for opportunities that would hopefully present themselves in the future.

The awkward questions came thick and fast and I supplied answers imperiously. What did it matter? I was never going to be considered as foreman material. I was far too young and inexperienced – wasn't I? Maybe next time eh? Imagine my total surprise when at the end of the interrogation, Mr Southworth smiled and told me that despite my brashness and over confidence he believed I possessed the raw attributes necessary to become part of the management team.

"Now go and get measured for your white coat and tell Mr Gates he will need to find a replacement tool setter very quickly as you start your new career on Monday," was his closing remark.

Chapter 17 – Blue Collar Days

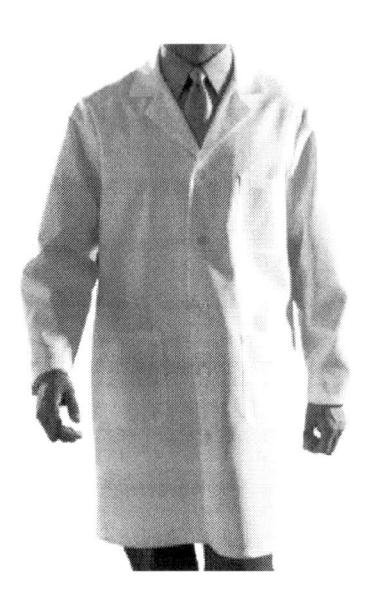

My new white coat with the blue collar fitted perfectly. The intention was that I should start my job as a foreman in the Comet Factory. However, there was an organizational problem at the Farington complex, which halted the move temporarily and so my first few weeks in my new supervisory role were spent in my own stomping ground of 104 department - a decision that turned out to be most injudicious.

It is difficult for any new foreman to be placed in a position where he is expected to supervise and give instructions to his previous peers and workmates. Why so, you may ask? Surely it must be easier to supervise in an area where all is known to you and of course there is no doubt that it has its advantages. Unfortunately these are outweighed by the fact that you also are aware of all the fiddles and malpractices that take place and as a responsible member of management what do you do about such goings on? I expressed my concern to a fellow foreman who had held the position for many years and was well respected by the workforce. His advice proved to be the best I could have hoped to receive in the circumstances. He told me that what knowledge I imagined was unique to me was actually well known by other members of the management team. Providing targets were being achieved and there were no serious breaches of company policy then it was best to ignore these indiscretions. This turned out to be wise council – Until that is, I did my first stint on the night shift.

The first few nights were uneventful and I ignored certain transgressions that had been going on for years including Tommy B nipping out of the window to buy fish & chips on a Friday night and the surreptitious card games that were played towards the end of the shift – and then disaster! It was about an hour from the end of the shift and as I was writing my report on the night's activities the office door was flung open and there stood a very senior member of management accompanied by 2 very concerned and serious looking policemen.

"Derek," said the manager, "These officers are trying to find John Doe (not his real name). Can you tell us where they might find him? His mother has been rushed into hospital very poorly and we need to locate him as soon as possible." My heart sank. John was one of our best machinists who regularly achieved his target production well before finishing time. Unfortunately he was in the habit of using this free time to snatch forty winks in one of the toilet cubicles. Everyone was aware of his rashness but as he always met his target the indiscretion was – shall we say – tolerated.

I was between a rock and a hard place, and this was before the expression had even been coined. Did I profess ignorance of his location or did I come clean and reveal his probable whereabouts. An idea came to me and I told those who were seeking him that I would ask the chap who worked on the next machine if he knew where 'John' was. Before there was the chance of a response I quickly exited the office, grabbed the first man I encountered and instructed him to go to the toilet block, locate the miscreant and tell him to report to my office ASAP. Moments later a somewhat sheepish operator entered the office proclaiming that he had been in the toilet but of course omitting to state the reason as to why he had been there.

And so a potentially uncomfortable situation had been avoided. John was taken to the local hospital and was relieved to find that his mum was not as poorly as first suspected. As luck would have it I emerged with 'brownie points' from all quarters. Shop floor personnel were happy in the way that I had managed what could have been a difficult situation and management, very unofficially of course held a similar view as if the truth had emerged there would have been no other recourse for John other than dismissal and the company would have lost one of it's best machinists. For me this was a valuable lesson hard learned but it proved that following convention to the letter without considering discretionary tactics did not always achieve the best or most desirable results.

It was during these early days of my supervisory career that we learned of the massive order that the company had received from Cuba for a sizeable fleet of over 600 buses. This had come at a time when the USA had imposed an embargo on trade with that country and was encouraging other countries to follow suit. However the majority of the Leyland workforce was overjoyed at the news, knowing that it would guarantee jobs for the foreseeable future.

Despite this apparent good news there always seems to be a dissolute minority who oppose anything that may be slightly controversial. I had witnessed a typical example of this form of opposition during my time as a machine tool setter. As well as manufacturing vehicles for the civilian markets, Leyland also supplied a range of fighting vehicles and ancillary parts. These component parts were identified on the manufacturing orders with the prefix FV and so the workforce were always aware when fighting vehicle parts were being manufactured.

On this particular day, the foreman had given me a manufacturing order for an FV component with the instruction to set it up on the first appropriate machine that became available. Big Jim's was the first to finish his previous job and so I approached him with the tools and order for completion of the part. As soon as Big Jim saw the FV identification he announced that as a pacifist he wanted nothing to do with assisting in making parts for 'killing machines' as he called them. Whilst respecting his principles I reminded him that he was working for a company that manufactured goods for a whole range of customers and even some of the parts not denoted FV could be supplied to the military.

It was no use. Big Jim was adamant he wanted nothing to do with making a part that was obviously destined for a fighting vehicle. The foreman was sent for and received a similar negative response. The senior foreman fared no better and so Big Jim was sent to the superintendent's office in a last ditch effort to make him see sense. A few moments later he emerged from the office, walked straight to his machine and asked me to set it up for the FV part. I was somewhat taken aback. Neither foreman nor senior foreman, despite long and protracted efforts, had managed to persuade Jim to forego his principles, yet two minutes with the super' and he was raring to go. Curiosity was killing me. I just had to ask him what had transpired in the big man's office.

"Well he explained it to me properly," answered Big Jim.

"What on earth did he say to you then?" I asked.

"He told me he was very sympathetic to my views and hoped that if I didn't go straight back and do the job I had been given, that I would find another job quickly and not to forget to pick up my cards on the way out!"

So it just goes to show that the direct approach at the opportune time to the right person sometimes works. Big Jim never protested again.

It was a similar story when the Cuban bus order was announced. We had a few operators that were either American, of American extract or had sympathetic views towards the Cuban embargo and gave notice that they would point blank refuse to work on any parts destined for this particular order. Our straight talking superintendent gathered the would-be dissidents together and gave them the Leyland equivalent of the Gettysburg Address. It went something like this:-

"Now look guys I never yet heard of a country that was invaded by bus and if it was ever attempted on the great US of A then I'm sure that the Yanks have enough firepower at their disposal to repel any such challenge before Fidel had time to say 'Fares Please'. However, seeing as you are all so interested in our buses, can I remind you that one passes the front gates very soon and takes you right past the Employment

Exchange (the forerunner of what we now know as the Job Centre). Now I suggest that you all return to your work stations, perform any job that is given to you and you can even sing 'God Bless America' while your carrying out your allotted tasks – That approach also worked.

The next few weeks were pretty uneventful until finally I was able to take up my position as a foreman in the Comet Shop. Despite my initial concerns of being a new boy among established supervisors I was relieved to see that I was not the only 'new kid on the block'. I had been instructed to report to a Mr Wilf Hulme, the senior foreman of the department. On entering his office I was met with a number of other tenderfoot foremen, Geoff, Allan, Bob and Tony, who like me, had been selected to undergo a quite revolutionary training programme. It transpired that the latest management policy was to ensure that all future supervisory promotions from the shop floor would not be unique to that single discipline but that candidates were also to be given 'hands on' experience in all aspects of industrial management. These secondments would include time to be spent in manufacturing planning, time study, procurement, industrial relations and material control.

Wilf Hulme was of the old school of supervisors who thought it 'daft' to appoint anyone to a supervisory role that had not spent at least half his working life with the tools of his trade. That being said Wilf was a well-respected foreman who certainly knew his job but did not suffer fools gladly. After giving us an introductory lecture he then placed each of his new acquisitions with an established foreman so that, in his words, they would hopefully learn enough about managing men and machines without bringing the factory to a halt in the process. I was placed with a very seasoned supervisor called Harry Palmer, a rather droll southerner who had come up from AEC many years previous. Harry possessed a rather laid back attitude to the job and yet he always seemed to meet his targets. He had a way of talking to the men he supervised which nearly always resulted in a positive result. He obviously wasn't short of a 'bob or two' and appeared to take every opportunity to bring out his oversize wallet which was always stuffed with bank notes of various denominations. In years past it was not the £1 and ten shilling notes that he was remembered for but rather the flashing of the large white 'fiver', which in earlier days was a banknote seldom seen by the working class. For this act alone the surname Palmer had been very seldom used and he was more affectionately and perhaps a little jealously known as 'Harry Fiver' by all who knew him.

My sojourn with Harry did not last long although the experience had been useful. Within the next few months I experienced secondments to virtually every section in the Comet Shop and with each move I learned a little more about the tricky business of front line supervision. I had believed that the array of manufacturing processes in North Works were numerous, but soon realized that the Comet Shop had an even greater range and as each day passed I became more confident in ensuring the smooth flow of work through the various manufacturing processes, although I realized that I still had much to learn in the even more delicate art of man management – particularly were shop stewards were concerned.

My first brush with Bill C occurred when he stopped me as I was carrying a couple of components round to the assembly area in order to complete an axle that was due to be shipped that day as part of an urgent order.

"Are you trying to put my members out of work?" was the plaintive cry that stopped me in my tracks. Now I had heard a little about Bill's somewhat fiery temperament but this was the first time we had ever crossed swords.

"Just trying to make sure an important order is completed on time Bill," I replied a little sheepishly.

"Aye, I can see that," he responded. "And the next thing you'll be recommending is a reduction in the men who are employed to do that job. It's like taking bread out of their mouths. I'll let it go this time as I know you are still wet behind the ears but don't let it happen again – You're not dealing with nig-nogs you know." I later learned that this was Bill's favourite, though politically incorrect terminology for anyone who behaved in such a way that didn't measure up to his principles.

As I passed the component parts to Steve Parr, my opposite number in the axle assembly area, I happened to mention my altercation with shop steward Bill. "Looks like you caught him on a good day," Steve laughingly replied. "Wait till he threatens your next misdemeanour with telling his members to down tools. That's his favourite gambit. Don't worry about it though. I think every supervisor in the factory has had that warning given to him by Bill but I've never seen it happen yet. He's full of bluster but despite his tough exterior he's really not a bad guy and you know exactly where you are with him. It's the sneaky ones you have to watch out for. They come over all friendly and cooperative but would drop you in it at the drop of a hat if it suited their purpose."

As the months passed I came to understand much better what Steve was telling me and before my next move along the management structure I got to know Bill very well and we came as close to becoming if not exactly friends but more like players in opposing teams that nurtured a mutual respect for each others role in the game. I also got to know Steve Parr better as well and was always grateful for his early advice. I also learned that he had been quite a well-known professional footballer in his early days and had actually played for Liverpool in the early 1950's, just before their real glory days. However, Steve was very modest and unassuming with regards to his football career and rarely spoke about his time as a fullback at Anfield. Over the next 25 years or so our career paths crossed on a number of occasions and we grew to be, and still are, very good friends.

There was one rather memorable though somewhat uncomfortable occasion in my early days as a foreman in the Comet Shop when a number of other young supervisors, myself included, incurred the wrath of our senior foreman, the aforesaid Wilf Hulme. At lunch times we had been in the habit of dining together in the works canteen, where a hearty 3-course meal could be purchased for a sum that would not even buy you a packet of crisps today. However, on the day in question we decided to have a change of venue and opted to visit the local 'chippy', which had a small dining area attached and was about a 5-minute walk from the factory.

On arriving at the chip shop we were confronted by shuttered doors on which hung a notice that told us that the establishment was 'Closed for Refurbishment.'

"Not to worry," said Tony confidently; "There's another chippy just a bit further down Golden Hill Lane." However, this 'little bit further' turned out to be a good half-mile and by the time we arrived at the doors, more than 50% of our allotted lunch time break had passed without yet a morsel passing our lips.

Now when the fates transpire against you they tend to do it in spades – There was a queue – right up the door. Unfortunately hunger had overtaken any thoughts of logic or reason and we decided unanimously that we must eat. With less than 5 minutes left of our lunch time we dashed from the shop, each clutching a steaming bag of fish & chips which we attempted to consume as we set off at a rather hot pace back to work.

We entered the big sliding doors of the Comet Shop nearly ten minutes after the start buzzer had sounded. As we made our furtive way towards the foremen's office, we thought at first that we had got away with our nefarious escapade – No such luck. There waiting for us at the office was – yes you've guessed it – the commanding figure of Wilf Hulme. If looks could kill we would all have expired on the spot. This however was only the start of our humiliation that day. He led us into the office and there we received the biggest dressing down that it was possible for one man to deliver without pausing for breath. Oh dear! If only that telling off could have signalled the end of our mortification. Unfortunately, within minutes virtually every worker in the factory learned of our transgressions and boy, did we suffer. For weeks after we were subject to taunts ranging from the slightly humorous to the down right derogatory. Believe me, it's an almost impossible task to deliver orders or instil discipline after such an unfortunate episode. However, it was a sobering lesson, hard learned but it obviously had the desired effect as all the miscreants on that unforgettable day rose to far higher management positions in the course of their employment at Leyland Motors.

It was while serving my stint as a foreman in the Comet Shop that I came very close to becoming a TV star. It was during this period that the BBC ran a documentary series about factory foremen and Leyland Motors was considered to be an ideal choice and location for the initial programme. The first I knew of the opportunity to feature in this documentary was when I was asked to go to the then works manager's office. As I made my way to Len Murray's domain that particular morning, I was of course wondering as to what had I done to elicit such a summons. The 'late after lunch' episode was long past so it couldn't be that. Nevertheless, I feared the worst.

As I entered the office, all I could see was a sea of strange faces. The fact that they were all smiling went someway to easing my fears of a worse case scenario. It was then that I spied Harry Rimmer, a long time fellow foreman who I had worked with during my time at North Works – He looked as bemused as I was feeling.

"Well, Harry and Derek, I expect you are wondering what this is all about, aren't you? Said the Manager. "Now don't look so worried the pair of you; I think you will like what I am about to tell you. It appears that the BBC is to make a documentary about supervision in the workplace and the pilot show will very likely be filmed at our very own factory. We were asked to select a couple of foremen to feature in the film, one with experience and one that was relatively new to the game, hence your attendance here today. Now, how do you both feel about that?

I admit I was gob smacked. Less than a year in the job and here I was being asked to play a part in a TV documentary. However, it was Harry who rose magnificently to the occasion and from his lengthy response he showed an artistic professionalism that I believe pretty well guaranteed his appearance in that first episode. As for myself, well I still fool myself in believing that my failure to pass the audition was because the camera didn't like me. However, if the truth were known, the real reason for the eventual rejection stamp was that I became totally tongue-tied when the cameras started rolling and I was asked as to what I thought were the main attributes required to being a good foreman. Harry, God bless him, had no such hang-ups and duly starred in a number of episodes and certainly did the sometimes difficult role of foreman very proud indeed.

In all I spent about six very enjoyable months as a foreman in the Comet Shop and some very firm friendships were formed that have continued up to the present day. As I have mentioned previously, I was one of a number of relatively young first line supervisors to be appointed under the revised management-training plan. The principle aim of this plan was to give foreman an insight into how all other manufacturing support departments operated and how they interacted with each other. It was therefore no surprise when I was informed that I was to be seconded to the Time Study Department as part of this training plan.

Chapter 18 – I Join the 'Enemy' Ranks

Now from earlier chapters you will have deduced that I had no great love for the activities of this department. As shop floor workers we were brain washed into believing that this particular section and the people who worked in it were the enemy. Through their machinations and duplicity, the ability for the sorely pressed worker to earn a decent bonus payment was severely restricted. So how was I likely to react when asked to serve within its ranks? My confidence at being able to perform as a functioning Time Study Engineer, or Rate Fixers as they were familiarly known was not enhanced on my first meeting with the head of the department, a Mr Len Holgate.

Now Mr Holgate (few people had the temerity to call him Len to his face) was without doubt from the exceedingly old school of managers. You realized this as soon as you entered the open plan office. His desk was situated at one end with all the TSE's desks set out uniformly in rows. It was just like a classroom set up, which was the effect that I'm sure Len was aiming for as it allowed him to keep his beady eye on his 'unruly' charges. If he thought there was too much gossip going on or - God forbid – laughter in the ranks, he would say nothing but rather raise his eyebrows and let out a noisy 'Harrumph' of displeasure, which usually had the desired effect. It took little imagination to visualize him a hundred or so years ago as a beadle in some grim workhouse or other.

Mind you, this was after all a first impression and as I got to know him better I realized that 80% of this gruff exterior was bluster and that he wasn't as bad an egg as everybody seemed to think. It was very much knowing which buttons to press and when. If you laughed at his inane jokes or listened intently to some of his boring reminisces then you were often rewarded by a glimpse of his softer side. On his better days and usually at lunch times, he would sometimes descend from his loftier plane and attempt to join in with the office banter. I remember well one crisp and bright autumnal day when he joined a group of us who were discussing the weekend's football matches. His opening contribution to the conversation was along the lines of "What a glorious day! What I wouldn't give for an open moor, a faithful dog and a sporting gun." Quick as a flash Norman replied, "I'm with you there boss but I think I would prefer an open road, a buxom blonde and a sporty jaguar." For a moment there was an uneasy silence before one by one we all started to laugh. Len let out one of his famous 'harrumphs' before stalking off, but I couldn't help but notice the twinkle in his eye.

Len was a confirmed bachelor and reminded me very much of a character from a Noel Coward play. Everything about him had echoes of the 1920's and 30's, from his hairstyle to his clipped moustache. I never knew what he did in his time away from work. It appeared that the highlight of his week was holding court with a like-minded circle of friends in the Kardomah Café, a rather up market 1930's style coffee house situated in Preston town centre.

There's no doubt that the policy of giving new supervisors a taster of all the manufacturing support processes was destined to pay long term dividends. Where previously I had held the Time Study department in pretty low esteem, when I became part of it I certainly saw things from a different perspective. Without boring you to rigid with the economics of the business, I learned that the department did have an important role to play in ensuring that the final cost of the product was competitive. The Time Study Department's role in this endeavour was to ensure that component parts were produced within the estimated cost/time scales.

My first venture down to the shop floor, equipped of course with my trusty stop watch, pencil, slide rule (don't forget these were pre-calculator days) and clipboard was to fix a production time on the machining of a small gear wheel from a steel forging. Having first been counselled by Mr Holgate, I knew the maximum time that I would be allowed to give the operator to ensure that it was produced within the prescribed limits. Having also been advised by a number of my new colleagues, I was also prepared, or so I thought, in the art of dealing with some of the dastardly tricks performed by the cunning machine operators in order to extract as much time from me as he possibly could (Who said 'by golly you've changed your tune).

"That was a very interesting performance Tommy," I said sarcastically to the operator as he completed his first demonstration. "Never really been fond of the fox trot though. How about changing those dancing shoes and stepping up to a quickstep for me and put the speeds and feeds up a notch or two while you're at it?" (Oh I'd been well versed in the art of rate fixer/operator banter, as you can no doubt tell). An hour or so later, after being accused of stealing bread from his children's mouths, having no time to visit the toilet (not Tommy's exact words but close enough) and much bazaar style haggling, we finally arrived at a mutually agreeable time for the job. I walked back to the office feeling quite proud of my negotiating skills – I'd priced the job at quite an amount lower than the original estimate. The almost inaudible 'harrumph' I received from Len when I informed him of my first 'fix' was praise indeed.

In all I spent about six months in the TS department, which included a short stint in the Manufacturing Planning section that allowed me to determine methods of manufacture as well as establishing times on a vast range of manufacturing procedures and without doubt improved my knowledge of this side of the business immensely. It was this phase in my career at Leyland Motors that led directly to an employment offer in the final years of my working life – but more of that in a later chapter. The day eventually came when I was called once again to the works manager's office.

"Seems like you've given a good account of yourself working for Mr Holgate," he told me. "So much so that he has asked me if I would allow him to offer you a permanent position in the department – What do you reckon?" There's no doubt I was flattered by the offer and told the manager I would certainly give it some serious consideration. He further informed me that should I choose to reject the offer I would be returning to North Works as a foreman.

"What about the management plan to give us all experience in the various manufacturing areas?" I asked him.

"We're shelving that plan at the moment as not all the respective managers are sold on the idea." As it happened the plan was not just shelved, it was discarded completely, which I considered a great shame as I had certainly benefited from the experience.

And so the next couple of days were spent in mulling over the offer of a permanent position as a Time Study Engineer. It was Margaret who finally convinced me that the position was not for me. She reminded me that since my secondment I had become very guarded in my responses to even simple questions as though I did not like to commit myself – and she was right. On reflection I believed that this was probably due to the guarded responses that one had to make when negotiating time allowances with operators. She reminded me of the response I had made that morning to her remark that it looked like another beautiful day.

"Well that all depends," was my guarded reply – Yes she was right, and I couldn't see the situation improving while I remained a TS engineer.

I think that Mr Holgate was genuinely disappointed when I informed him that although I was flattered by his offer, I believed that my future career at Leyland Motors lay in the province of man management rather than time study. He was very understanding and thanked me for the time that I had spent in his department. He also informed me that if I ever changed my mind he would be more than happy to take me back as a TS engineer. I told him that although I believed that my future lay elsewhere, I appreciated the offer and thanked him for giving me the opportunity to learn a little about time and motion study. I handed in my stopwatch and clipboard, exchanged my plain white coat for one with a blue collar and set off once more to the North Works.

Chapter 19 – North Works - The Magnet

As I walked down the central passageway of North Works, I mused that it was now 15 years since I first set foot in this, the original Leyland Motors factory as a very timorous apprentice. I hadn't done badly for someone with a less than inspiring education and even then I wondered where the next 35 years or so would take me. My reverie was disturbed as I reached the entrance to my old stomping ground - 104 department. There I bumped into a fellow foreman, George Astley. He informed me that my second stint as a supervisor at North Works would be in 102 department, which was another miscellaneous machine shop that housed the majority of the factories internal and external grinding machines.

There I spent a fairly uneventful but nonetheless enjoyable 3 or 4 months and began to warm to my position as a foreman. Perhaps this had something to do with the workforce there. Most of the operators were well over the first flush of youth and asked for nothing more than to be allowed to get on with their allocated tasks, which I was more than happy to go along with. Weekly targets were met comfortably and although making firm friendships was not encouraged, I believe a bond of mutual respect was forged – Until yet another fateful day dawned.

Fred was a fitter in the last 12 months of his working life. His job consisted mainly of fitting ancillary parts to various types of shafts. It was a simple task, not strenuous and just perfect for a 64-year-old. Fred's bench was situated in a corner of the workshop with the component parts arriving in containers known as 'drop boxes' and so designed that they could be stacked one on top of the other. I had noticed that from time to time a certain zealous labourer would stack the boxes around Fred in such a way that it was difficult for him to leave his bench without first negotiating the said boxes.

Realizing that this was an accident just waiting to happen, I instructed another member of the labouring team to create a passageway by delineating the same with white lines. This worked well for a time until the fateful day that 'zealous labourer', having no other free space to deposit a box of components, dropped it plum in Fred's passage (sorry! – I'll rephrase that – In the passageway created for Fred). Sod's law was definitely operating that day – in spades. Fred, carrying a mug of hot tea back to his work station, clambered across the offending box – and fell awkwardly, breaking his wrist and a couple of fingers in the process. The injuries were so serious that poor

Fred was unable to work again during the few months left before his retirement. The net result of this unfortunate accident was an industrial courts case that Fred, although somewhat reluctant to do so, had been advised to pursue.

Many lessons were learned on the day that the case went to court. One aspect of the eventual proceedings was a tenet that I hold dear to this day. Where the law is concerned it's not always a matter of who's right and who's wrong but which party has the smartest lawyer. Fred had been offered a fairly respectable out of court settlement but had been advised by the trade union law team to reject it, as they were confident that they could secure for him a much larger payout in the courtroom.

As the foreman of the department where the accident occurred, I was called to give evidence on behalf of Leyland Motors. Prior to going into the witness box I was briefed by the company's representative, a QC no less who I'm pretty sure, if memory serves me right, went by the name of Sir Henry Rose. He informed me that as the first line supervisor I would probably get an intense grilling from the plaintiff's counsel, which would probably include an accusation of negligence for not ensuring that the passageway, that I had been instrumental in creating, was kept clear. There were a number of other disconcerting points raised that made me feel more like a criminal myself than just a mere witness and I began to dread my appearance in the box.

However, Sir Henry had not risen to the legal rank of a QC through lack of attention to detail, for as well as alerting me to all the tricky questions I was likely to be faced with, he also advised me as how best to answer them. He also added that he would be on hand to interject if he felt I was floundering. It was therefore with somewhat mixed feelings that I sat outside the courtroom later that day, along with just one other witness for the defence, waiting to be called to give my account. Seated opposite us were at least half a dozen of Fred's co-workers who no doubt would be called upon to give their accounts of the accident.

I think it is only fair to state that at this point in the proceedings, I believed that Fred had a pretty good case against the company and would be compensated accordingly. Suffice it to say that as a result of the case Fred was awarded a sum that was about 50% of the out of court figure previously offered. This meant that technically he had 'lost' the case and it also meant that the AEU trade union that was representing him would now have to pay the legal costs of the hearing. Surprised? You bet I was – But now let me tell you as to just how this extraordinary settlement was reached.

After being called and having given my honest and I believe accurate account of the accident, with I must add little interjection from Fred's union appointed lawyer (A fresh faced nervous young fellow who looked and acted as if was straight out of law school), I was allowed to remain in the courtroom. What I heard next was truly 'Rumpolesque' and would have graced any TV courtroom drama. Now one of the tasks that Sir Henry had asked of me in the briefing was to draw a sketch of the area where the accident had occurred. He was very insistent that the sketch should portray, as accurately as I could recall, Fred's workbench, the recently created passageway and the stacked up boxes.

Fred was the first to be called to give his account of the accident. Sir Henry, using my original sketch as a guide, asked Fred to mark the spot where he had fallen. He then feigned great empathy with the victim of the accident and from his tone Fred must have thought he had gained an ally – It was then that the legal sabre first flashed. Sir Henry remarked with great sympathy that it was very fortunate that Fred had now retired and was not reliant on a wage to keep himself and his dependents – Fred agreed. (Slash! – That's a few hundred off the sum claimed). He then added that as he no longer needed to work his injury would cause him no hindrance – Fred again nodded his agreement. (Swish! Another 'grand' gone), and finally by his demeanour and pleasant outlook that he was suffering no pain due to his unfortunate accident. (Slice – bang goes another significant amount). By the time he had finished with poor Fred, Sir Henry had almost made it appear that having the accident was a blessing rather than a curse. However our conniving QC was just getting into his legal stride.

The plaintiff's witnesses were then called in one by one and I noticed that Sir Henry had made a number of copies of my original sketch. He proceeded to ask each witness the same set of questions, marking each positional answer onto a fresh drawing. The questions asked were along the lines of; where did the accident occur and where did he fall? What, if anything was he carrying? Was he leaving or returning to his workstation? When the procession of witnesses finally came to an end, each giving their interpretation of events, Sir Henry then launched into his defence speech on behalf of the company.

I was both dismayed and yet overawed by what followed. Using the collection of Fred's and the witnesses' drawings, he virtually tore the case apart. No two drawings were alike as to where Fred had actually fallen, what he was carrying or in which direction he had been travelling. This contradictory 'evidence', coupled with Fred's earlier statement gave the judge little choice but to make the somewhat derisory award that he did – and I could see that he wasn't exactly overjoyed with the decision that he had been forced to make.

On reflection I think I could have made a better fist of the way that the trade union lawyer had handled the case on Fred's behalf. In the de-briefing that followed even Sir Henry admitted that he was surprised at the lack of 'fight' and counter argument from his fellow brief. However, as I remarked earlier, there were salutary lessons to be learned from this legal encounter that served me well throughout my time as both a foreman and a manager as you will see in a later chapter.

The rest of my time in 102 was fairly uneventful apart from a couple of rather amusing incident that occurred when I was asked (make that told) to do a turn on the nightshift. Most of the departments had a compliment of machinists working this shift and it was thought adequate for just the one foreman, along with the nightshift superintendent, to supervise the whole factory. This wasn't as difficult as it may at first appear, as all jobs were prearranged from the dayshift. All that was required from the nightshift supervision was to ensure that this work was completed.

Although the number of operators to oversee was relatively small, the geographical area I had to cover in my supervisory duties was pretty vast. On the whole the discipline of the workforce was good and apart from the odd maverick they gave me very few problems. From my time as a turner on the nightshift I was pretty aware of all the little tricks that the men got up to; nothing that serious of course but there was one discipline that Joe N, the night superintendent, was keen on stamping out and that was dining before the buzzer sounded for the official break. It was impossible to cover the whole factory and so I made a point of visiting one of the workshops per night in a random sequence. It worked pretty well and the brave few who dared to start eating their 'bagging' before the official time soon realized there was little point as they never knew where I would 'pop up' next.

On this particular night I decided to pay a rare visit to the Tool Room, where Harry, my father-in-law just happened to work. Of the half dozen or so men that laboured in this particular area I noticed a couple of them sitting down with their backs to me, tucking into their dinners. You've probably guessed by now that – yes – one of them was Harry. "Enjoying that are you?" I casually remarked. Without turning round to ascertain who had interrupted his meal, he replied, "I am so just go away and let me get on with it." I hasten to add that these were not his exact words but the meaning was pretty much the same. "Now what would your Annie say if she heard you being so rude to your son-in-law." There was what I suppose you would call a pregnant pause before he slowly turned and realized who had accosted him. The look of guilt on his face was a picture and it didn't help when his workmates started laughing and making comment regarding his 'crime'. I tut-tutted, walked slowly away, desperately trying to stifle my own laughter. Do you know, I don't think that he ever quite forgave me?

The other amusing episode also involved Harry. With the benefit of hindsight it was very funny but at the time the incident almost ended in fisticuffs. Harry was a machine tool fitter whose job was to ensure that any machine breakdowns that might occur during the shift were quickly attended to. In this task another fitter who went by the name of Deegan partnered him. Now although Harry's partner did have a first name, everyone knew him as just 'Deegan' He was a short and stocky redheaded guy and known throughout the factory for his somewhat fiery disposition. Deegan had an opinion on just about everything, particularly if the subject was controversial. Most of the time he was wrong (some say deliberately just to promote controversy) but such was his reputation that very few dared argue to vehemently with him. Unfortunately, one of the 'few' was father-in-law, Harry and the discussions and subsequent arguments that took place between the pair were legendary and often attracted quite an audience of fellow workers.

On the night in question I just happened to be passing the Tool Room and could not help but notice the raised voices that came from within. As I passed through the doors I was met with the sight of Harry and Deegan, nose-to-nose, arms waving wildly, both very red in the face and trading insults and obscenities with each other. Using all my supervisory powers I stepped in between them and enquired as to just what had happened to stir up such a verbal maelstrom.

"The stupid bugger has only gone and put my dinner in the oven," screamed an over wrought Harry.

"What's the problem with that?" I replied. "Seems like a nice gesture to me," I added in an attempt to calm the situation down.

"Nice gesture my arse - I was on a bloody salad tonight – that's what wrong – and he knew it as well," responded Harry indignantly.

"I had forgotten that you had told me earlier," said Deegan with feigned meekness. "It was just habit, and anyway I've told him he can half of mine."

"Curry! That's what he has – stinking curry. He knows I can't stand the bloody stuff. He's just trying to wind me up as usual" Harry yelled angrily; and doing a pretty good job of it I mused, trying desperately to keep a straight face. It was then that the solidarity of the British workman shone through and all within earshot (by now quite a crowd had gathered) offered to share their 'bagging' with him.

With order just about restored I made to absent myself from the proceedings and had almost reached the large rubber doors when a further uproar of laughter mixed with angry expletives halted me in my tracks. As I somewhat reluctantly returned to the fray it was to observe the 'cad' Deegan, a big grin splitting his ruddy countenance, holding aloft the dish containing Harry's salad, which had obviously been nowhere near the oven. Poor Harry didn't know whether to laugh or cry at this unexpected turn of events but I could tell by the look in his eye that revenge was definitely on the cards, and to this day no one is quite sure how, a few nights later, a fake but very realistic looking plastic turd found its way into Deegan's lunch tin…

It was shortly after this long talked about incident when, once again I was given a change of scenery. 105 was the machine shop where most of the milling and drilling was carried out in the North Works. Eric Ryding, one of the two foremen who supervised in this area, was taken ill and I was asked to fill the breach in his absence. That was fine by me as I relished the opportunity to gain as much experience as possible with regards to the various manufacturing processes. The one drawback however was that I would be working alongside Jack Smith. Now Jack was definitely a foreman from the old school and had seen and dealt with it all. What Jack didn't know about milling and drilling was not worth knowing and now I had the opportunity to learn from the master himself. This of course was on the plus side of my latest appointment – but there was a down side. Jack was a strict disciplinarian and did not suffer fools gladly, whomever they might be or whatever position they might hold. Initially he looked on me as a total supervisory greenhorn, believing that anyone under the age of 40 was not equipped to deal with the trials and tribulations of running a machine shop.

My first few weeks working alongside Jack were not easy. He seemed reluctant to pass on his vast store of knowledge and appeared to judge every action I took with disdain or disapproval. It was somewhat unfortunate that it took a serious industrial accident for him to realize that maybe there was more to this apparent rookie than he had initially given credence for. The scream was heard all around the department. Somebody had obviously been hurt. I happened to be at the other end of the machine shop at the time but knew that as the joint supervisor for the area it was part of my remit to investigate the reason for such an agonized cry of pain.

The scene that met me was straight from a horror movie set. A young milling machine operator had been caught up in the cutters of his machine. It appeared that he had been attempting to remove a build up of 'swarf' or metal shavings from the cutters when they had caught on the loose sleeve of his overalls and dragged his arm into the machine. The razor sharp blades had inflicted terrible injuries to his arm and when I arrived at the dreadful scene it was to witness Jack Smith, who had somehow managed to stop the machine, thus preventing the revolving blades from inflicting further mutilating injuries to the now semiconscious operator and was attempting to both support him and staunch the remorseless blood flow from the terrible wound.

A number of fellow workers at the scene appeared to be traumatized by what they were witnessing and seemed unable or unwilling to assist. I must confess that my initial thoughts were to flee from the carnage as fast as I could. However, from somewhere I managed to find the courage and fortitude to help Jack. It's amazing how one reacts when the adrenalin kicks in and without even thinking I whipped the belt from my trousers and fastened it as tight as I could around the poor man's upper arm. The blood flow slowed to a mere trickle and I realized I had done the right thing.

Just minutes later, although at the time it seemed like an eternity, came the welcoming sight of the North Work's medical staff to relieve us. Our white coats were now completely red as Jack and I were led from the scene. It was an experience that haunts me to this day and yet the outcome was surprisingly favourable. The surgical team at the local hospital managed to save the unfortunate operator's arm and although he did suffer some loss of use of the limb he was eventually able to resume his career.

From that day on Jack and I became best buddies and he couldn't do enough to help me at furthering my knowledge in the finer arts of milling and drilling. However, the incident had left its psychological mark on me and I began to dread passing over the threshold of the department at the commencement of each shift and realized that I needed to get out of 105 and probably North Works altogether. It was soon after that the opportunity to do so arrived.

Chapter 20 – The 'Headless Wonder'

I had learnt through the supervisory grapevine that the recently opened New Engine Factory, situated within the Spurrier Works, was looking for a foreman to assist an old colleague of mine, Don Peddie. Frank Nelson, the superintendent of this new factory, had appointed Don, a fellow foreman from my early North Works days, to assist in commissioning the first manufacturing line in this new state-of-the-art plant. The product to be manufactured using a continuous flow-line concept was the newly designed and revolutionary AEC V8 Engine block.

The ensuing interview with Frank went very well as we shared very similar views as to how best to run a newly commissioned factory and were equally excited to be in at the birth of what promised to be very successful and groundbreaking product. Within days I was offered the position of foreman and was very happy to accept. I had of course to serve a period of notice at the North Works until a suitable replacement foreman was appointed and it was with mixed feelings when the day came for me to leave the 'old girl' who had been chiefly responsible for the knowledge that I had gained both as a tradesman and supervisor…

This new purpose built plant had also been commissioned for the production of the major component parts for the even more innovative power source – the 0/500 engine or the 'Headless Wonder' as it came to be known. Much has been said and written by engineers far more qualified than I about both of these engines. Unfortunately very little of the publicity they received was either positive or complimentary and subsequently both engines failed as the new revolutionary product that Leyland was so desperately searching for in the late 1960's and 70's in an effort to stave of growing international competition. For my part and of course with the benefit of hindsight, I still believe that both engines could have achieved 'world beater' status if only there had been more development and testing time afforded to the radical designs instead of the insane rush to get them into the marketplace before they were proven.

Well that's the politics out of the way; now I will tell you more about the stimulating times experienced by all the workforce in the subsequent manufacturing of the component parts. The V8 engine block was the only part of the AEC designed engine to be made in the new factory. However, for the 0/500 engine it was a different story. All the main engine components were to be produced here including the engine block itself, crankcases, crankshafts, connecting rods, tappet blocks and bearing caps. Each part was to be manufactured on a dedicated flow line using state of the art machinery designed specifically for the task.

Even in these early stages of setting up the specialized flow lines the gremlins were certainly playing their part in holding up production. The commissioning of the more complex machines was taking far longer than anticipated, despite the best efforts of all concerned. As the weeks passed, both staff and shop floor personnel were under daily pressure to get the various flow lines up and running. The situation was not helped when an official opening day, to which the TV and national press were invited to attend, was announced. We were nowhere near ready for such a visit and though all the machines were in 'one off' working order when nursed along and had produced enough parts to set up a small assembly area, they had never run for the sustained periods for which they had been originally designed.

It was the day before the visit when in sheer desperation it was decided to pass component parts through the high profile machines that had already been rejected for a variety of reasons. It was assumed (wrongly as it turned out) that press and TV personnel as non-engineers and suitably fed and dined would be none the wiser and at least they would see parts being automatically transferred from one machining stage to another.

The TV crews had set up extra bright lights and the cameras were rolling. The press boys were busily scribbling in their notebooks whilst still cameras were busily clicking away. It was at that moment when Wilf Thompson our factory Manager at the time walked up to me, accompanied by an elderly journalist who had obviously seen it all before and though well in his 'cups' enquired of me as to why there were drilled and tapped holes in a crankcase that had just emerged from a machining station that was positioned well before the one that performed the actual drilling and tapping?

I prayed that the ground beneath my feet would open thus giving me an avenue to escape and evade the question. When no such miracle occurred, I knew it was time to think fast.

"Well spotted sir," I replied, in a desperate attempt to massage his ego. "That one happens to be a rework as the last stage of machining was incomplete due to a broken cutter and as this is a flow line, all reworks must be loaded at the start of the line and transported through to the required machining stage." The factory manager smiled, obviously satisfied with my reply and walked away. However, the world-weary journalist was not as easily duped. He eyed me quizzically and remarked in an easy laconic tone,

"Must be some hell of a machining stage that last one; better than Lazarus I reckon if it can resurrect a part that has 'scrap' written on the side!" I smiled wanly but before I had the opportunity to reply he added, "But hey, well done young fellow, I reckon you'll go far – ever thought of becoming a journalist?"

We just about got away with it. The TV and press were reasonably kind and even 'Hard-Bitten from Fleet Street' gave us a reasonable write-up. The following morning, Frank Nelson, our superintendent told me that the factory manager had been impressed by the way I had conducted myself – even though he realized I was lying through my teeth in an effort to save the situation…

Eventually we did manage to get all the manufacturing lines up to a decent level of production and it was time to add to the specialist crews of operators who had, I believe, performed minor miracles in achieving this status. Don and I were given the task of recruiting the additional staff required and as the New factory products were viewed as somewhat innovative and prestigious there was no shortage of volunteers. The interview sessions were rewarding for two especial reasons, one, they allowed us to select the best possible operators, much to the chagrin of the departments who were losing their services and from a personal point of view for the opportunity that it gave me in the art of interviewing.

Our selection criterion was to aim for an eclectic mix of younger operators and those with more machining experience. This we were able to achieve and the combination worked well and I have no doubts that if the two engine designs had proven more successful and the specialised machinery had performed as efficiently as the workforce then the New Engine Factory would have proved to be a jewel in the Leyland Motors crown. However, there turned out to be a sporting as well as a works related benefit from employing a mainly younger workforce. This was realized when the time came for selecting teams for the annual departmental cricket competition and we believed that in the New Engine Factory we had the foundation of a team that could certainly challenge for the honour of being Leyland Motor's champions – But more of that in the next chapter.

By now I'm sure you will have realized that certainly in those early days the fates had appeared to have conspired in a number of ways to frustrate both management and shop-floor operatives in their attempts to manufacture quality components on a commercial basis. This 'bad luck' was no more apparent than with the 'first off' of the AEC V8 Engine Block. Under extreme pressure from senior management, Don and his machine tool setter Bill Baxter had pulled out all the stops in an effort to achieve an almost impossible deadline that had been set for them. It was inevitable that under such unrelenting pressure corners would be cut in an effort to achieve the target date and errors would occur. So how then did the dreaded gremlins strike? A hole was drilled out of position in the block, which under normal conditions would have rendered the component unfit for purpose. Such action as this of course would have meant that the target date set would have been impossible to achieve.

Foolishly, but with every good intention, Don and Bill agreed that they could plug the hole in such a way that it would be virtually impossible to detect – Unfortunately they had failed to take into account the eagle eye of a very senior member of management. With great ceremony and in the presence of company directors and senior design personnel, the completed Engine block went on display at the end of the machine line. Don and Bill stood proudly as they were praised for their efforts in meeting the target date. It was at that moment that a shaft of sunlight struck the engine block. Quite appropriate you might think to highlight the efforts in producing the goods on time. Unfortunately the unexpected beam exposed the very slight and almost imperceptible difference in colour of the parent material of the engine block and the metal used to plug the offending hole – And who should spot it? Why none other than Ian Black, the Quality Director.

The inquest was short and bloody. Don, being the gentleman that he was, took immediate responsibility for the attempted repair, exonerating Bill from any involvement and was subsequently, and I believe, very harshly punished. Within days he was relieved of his position as senior foreman and informed that he would never again be allowed to oversee in a manufacturing area and was consequently given a minor supervisory role in the material stores. To this day I believe that the sentence was extreme and in any other circumstances would not have resulted in such ruthless castigation. There were two losers that day; Don lost his confidence and Leyland lost the services of a bloody good machine shop foreman.

For every loser I suppose there has to be a winner and though it was not under ideal circumstances, a replacement foreman, Reg Eastham, an established supervisor from the No 8 Machine Shop was recruited and I was appointed senior foreman with the immediate task of producing a pristine V8 engine block. As cruelly as the 'Gods of Manufacturing' had frowned on Don they certainly smiled on me. The engine block following the ill-fated one was only a matter of days from completion and it was with huge sighs of relief all round that, after a very thorough and searching inspection it was eventually declared serviceable, and handed over for final assembly.

I was also appointed senior foreman over the 0/500 assembly area much to the initial disgust of Arthur Cumpstey, the line foreman, whose initial assessment of someone with virtually no previous knowledge of assembly protocol was less than favourable. However, after a few weeks of working together and demonstrating that through my senior status I was able to assist him more than he had originally realized we eventually forged a good working relationship. Jumping the gun slightly I am happy to relate that Arthur himself became a more than able assembly superintendent. It was with great sorrow that soon after the factory closure I learned that he had died in very tragic circumstances.

One of the first tests of my new senior position was surprisingly not works related. It occurred during the height of the 'troubles' in Northern Ireland. There had been a couple of bomb scares in the local area so it came as no great surprise when, just after commencement of the afternoon shift, I received a phone call from the head of factory security informing me that they had received an anonymous call regarding an explosive device that had been planted in the 0/500 factory. He added that it was probably a hoax but nevertheless to be on the safe side the building had to be evacuated immediately.

I speedily informed Reg and Arthur and between us we managed to get everyone out and well clear of the factory building in double quick time. We were feeling quite proud of ourselves, especially on receiving high praise from the security chief on our alacrity.

"Where's little Richard?" (No! not that one) the cry rang out. Now Richard, or as he was more familiarly known as, Dick, was an elderly labourer whose regular lunchtime routine was to eat his 'bagging' and then settle down in his little cubbyhole under the toilet stairs for a little siesta. It would not be the first time that Dick had 'missed' the starting buzzer but trust it to be on this particular day for him to oversleep.

"I'll go and get him," I said making for the factory door.

"You will not enter that building under any circumstances Mr Rogerson," boomed the security chief. "If anyone goes in it will be me and my team."

"But you don't know where his little hidey-hole is situated. I do and we can be in and out in two minutes flat." Now I'm pretty sure that if this situation had happened today, poor Dick would have been condemned by H & S legislation to remain where he was. Fortunately for him common sense still had a part to play in the early '70's and with a curt nod the chief motioned me to follow him into the factory.

I don't think that poor Dick could have been any more alarmed if the bomb had gone off. We burst through the little door, grabbed him by both arms and half carried him out of the building. A resounding cheer from the assembled workforce met us and Dick still had no idea what it was all about. However, his usual cheery grin faded fast when I explained to him the true circumstances surrounding his rescue.

By this time all the emergency services had arrived at the scene and were evaluating the situation. After about an hour or so they decided to enter the building and after an exhaustive search where nothing suspicious was found, they declared that it was now safe for the workforce to enter the building once more. As the security chief was thanking me for my help, a high-ranking member of the constabulary who, with stentorian voice coupled with a very stern countenance said that officially our actions were stupid, foolhardy and reckless approached us. His face then softened as he added, "But then again so were the 'D-Day' landings!"

With the factory now as operational as it was ever destined to be, the factory manager decreed that the workforce, in line with all other operatives at the Spurrier Factory site, should be paid by results. Knowing that I had a working knowledge of time study methods and in agreement with my old boss Len Holgate, I was asked to work out some form of piecework or bonus scheme for the various production lines. It took many weeks before a system that was agreeable to both management and the workforce was thrashed out. It worked very well and all parties were delighted by the results. It was also very frustrating as the incentive system was successful when the lines were operational, but unfortunately due to the unreliability of many of the more complex machines, it achieved only limited success. I believe that it was this extra involvement in setting up a workable incentive system that assisted me in becoming a front-runner for a superintendent's position that was about to be announced.

Dean Bell was at this time superintendent of the No 8 Machine Shop. This manufacturing area had originally been built as part of the Spurrier Factory complex and commissioned by the MoD for the production of Centurion Tanks in 1953, which were successfully deployed in the Korean War. The factory had then been handed over to Leyland Motors in 1956 and took on its present name in honour of the co-founder of the company, Sir Henry Spurrier.

Dean, another old colleague from earlier days, had just been appointed manager of the North Works complex and his considerable shoes had now to filled. However, No 8 shop had grown significantly and was apparently one of the largest manufacturing plants under one roof in Europe. It was therefore considered to large for one superintendent to manage successfully. Les Southworth, the works director, decided to divide the shop between two superintendents and no one was more surprised than me to learn that I was a candidate for one of the positions.

However, the 0/500 factory held one final hurrah for me. It came not on the factory floor but on a cricket field. Our team had reached the final – and I was down to play!

Before I close this particular chapter, I believe I should mention that it was during my early years in the 0/500 factory that the big strike took place. For a number of years there had been unrest on the shop floor due to a number of pay issues but principally to the perceived unfairness of the old and outmoded piecework arrangement. This came to a head in 1969 when the then Works Convenor called a strike that affected all the hourly paid workers in the 5 Leyland plants. It lasted for a number of weeks and ended on a compromise that would eventually improve the inequitable bonus scheme.

Although it was deemed a strike that bore satisfactory results for the shop floor personnel, I personally believe that these were short term and that it was somewhat of a pyrrhic victory. The hourly paid did eventually receive a fairer pay structure but at the cost of lost reputation to the company. To date the Truck & Bus division had not been tarred with the same industrial action brush that had affected other BMC plants and no major strike had ever affected production at Leyland. However, competition from European manufacturers was beginning to affect Leyland's order books and I believe that the strike, although not totally responsible, was at least the catalyst for one of the nails in the coffin that eventually contributed to its demise.

There will no doubt be those among my many millions (hopefully) of readers who do not share this sentiment - and that is fine – I stress that the above is my own opinion of the incident and I make no apology for including it in this book.

Chapter 21 – HOWZAT? - Shop Competitions

As I mentioned earlier, the inter-departmental competitions set up by the LMSAC (Leyland Motors Social & Athletic Club) were very well supported throughout the company. These competitions took many forms and most popular sports and pastimes were covered. However the two that attracted the most attention were undoubtedly the football and cricket competitions. Virtually every factory, office, shop, section or line entered a team and great rivalries, keen but friendly were the order of the day.

Being a lover of both football and cricket and despite having less than average ability in either codes, I nevertheless always enjoyed taking part in these competitions. It mattered little whether we finished victors or the vanquished as the games were always enjoyable and at the end of play invariably resulted in a visit to either the LMSAC bar or the Eagle & Child where a pint or three would be sunk during the inevitable inquest.

In those early days I can never remember getting much further than the second or third rounds of the competitions, apart from one memorable occasion in 1964 while I was working at the North Works. It just so happened that scattered through the many departments there were a number of guys who were pretty good exponents of the 'beautiful game'. Ken Woods was a great goalkeeper and was currently playing for

114

Lytham Town football club. There was Dick Entwhistle, a rock of a defender who had been on Preston North End's books, John Rotherham was also a defender of renown; George Pails although small of stature was a midfielder to be reckoned with and the Robinson twins were a handful for any defence. There were others of equal prowess whose names unfortunately escape me but there was no denying that the North Works could field a pretty decent squad in 1964.

Of course I could never hope to gain a place in such illustrious company on the field but at least I got the next best position off it, that of assistant manager. Jack Mather, having being an ex-semi professional had the distinction of leading the squad but much to my surprise he asked me if I would assist him in his role. I was naturally delighted to accept the position and fancied myself as perhaps being another Peter Taylor supporting our own Brian Clough. If he had told me at the time that one of my duties would be to carry the bucket and sponge on match days I'm not sure if I would have been quite so enthusiastic.

Our progress through the earlier rounds was majestic. Up to the semi-final the team had scored a bagful of goals while Ken Woods had as yet to retrieve the ball from his own net. The semis though brought on sterner opposition. The team we faced were a robust, rough and tough set of blokes and gave our lads a real bruiser of a game. Ken, for the first time had to pick the ball from the net although he didn't have far to go. He had been deposited there along with the ball in a tussle that these days would have resulted in at least a yellow card. But in the end class told and to the delight of every employee at the North Works we found ourselves in the final.

This game was staged on the Thurston Road ground in the shadow of the now long gone LMSAC building. Excited supporters of both teams surrounded all four sides of the pitch. We were up against (if memory serves me right) a strong team of young guys from the various drawing offices whose progress to the final had been even more impressive than ours – and they started clear favourites.

It was a terrific game, a mixture of brawn and brains and I was called on to administer the magic sponge on numerous occasions. The score was locked at two apiece as the game entered its final phase. George Pails made a darting run down the wing leaving desperate defenders in his wake; centred the ball to perfection and there was young 'Robbo' waiting at the far post to head it in – The cup was ours.

Celebrations in the upstairs bar of the LMSAC in the aftermath of our famous victory went long into the night and there were more than a few sore heads that clocked into work the following morning. Up to that moment I don't believe that North Works had ever won the football cup and to the best of my knowledge, after 1964, they never won it again – A bit like the England team a couple of years later.

Despite playing in lesser teams on many occasions over the ensuing years, I had to wait quite some time before I was to take part in another final – but this time it was to be on the cricket field. As I mentioned in the previous chapter the 0/500 Engine Factory now employed a number of young guys who were handy with both the 'willow' and the 'leather'. Three names that stand out even now were Michael Howard, who had played for Lancashire Colts and was our star batsman. Alex Smith, who was currently playing for the Leyland Fox Lane Cricket Club was our demon bowler and Derek Dell was our resolute and perfect all-rounder.

The rest of the team was comprised of regular cricketers and though I was certainly not in the same class I managed to creep into the squad, usually as 12th man. The team's progress to the final was fairly uneventful and all our matches were won with a degree of comfort and it was no surprise to find that when the day of the final dawned against a team drawn from various drawing offices, the 0/500 Engine Shop started as clear favourites. When the team sheet was posted a couple of days before the match, I was a little surprised but very pleased to find that I had been selected.

The day of the final dawned clear and bright and as the team made it's way to the field we were all in good heart but perhaps a little carried away by our favourites tag. We won the toss and elected to field with the clear certainty that whatever score the opposition posted, our team were talented enough to pass it. Unfortunately runs came steadily and wickets fell infrequently and in a 20 over match our adversaries ran up a pretty decent score. This rather daunting score line was helped in no small measure by my contribution. I bowled two very indifferent overs with a return of no wickets for plenty and even managed to drop a catch on the last ball of our opponent's innings.

Our captain, Mick Howard however was still upbeat as in an attempt to console me he said that I was not to worry as being last man in it was unlikely that I could cause further damage as by then the match would be won. Our innings turned out to be the reverse of our opponents as wickets fell steadily and runs came infrequently. I heard the dreaded shout of 'Howzat' and the umpire's finger rose slowly skyward. That was the 9th wicket down making it my turn to bat and still a dozen or so runs short of the target that would bring us victory. There were still a couple of overs to go and Alex, my fellow batsman, who himself had rattled up a good score, advised me not to play rashly and where possible leave it him to get the runs needed.

Unfortunately this was not to be a 'Vitai Lampada' moment for the 0/500 shop. I did however manage to claw back a little self-respect by scoring a few runs. Sadly and with three required to win off the last ball, Alex struck out defiantly – and was caught just inside the boundary rope – but at least I carried my bat. The cup was presented to the worthy winners by the Spurrier Works Manager at the time, Wilf Thompson and both victors and vanquished repaired to the LMSAC club where pints were supped and we consoled ourselves with the thought that there was always next year – But for at least one member of the losing team this was not to be. That Person? – Me!

Chapter 22 – Climbing The Ladder

I suppose that in hindsight you could say that 1972/73 were probably the best productive years for the 0/500 Engine Factory. That was certainly true of the machine shop area. Most of the components manufacturing lines were running as smoothly as they ever would and little stockpiles of finished parts began to accumulate as the continuing running problems with the finished engine was constantly affecting the rate of assembly as various modifications were introduced in an effort to produce a quality engine.

It was during 1973, with a new factory manager in place, Ken Bosonnet, that I learned I was being considered as one of the two new superintendents that were to be appointed in the No 8 Machine Shop. As I touched on in an earlier chapter, Dean Bell, the previous head of this expanding workshop, was moving on and his empire was now considered to large for one man to run successfully. The other candidate for the position was Tom Barber, a university graduate. Although Tom had little supervisory experience at this time, he had shown that the prospect of running a large machine shop was just the experience he needed to make him an all round professional engineer.

We both underwent pretty searching interviews and we were both successful. Tom was offered the post of superintendent over Miscellaneous Machining while I was put in charge of the Flow Lines due to experience gained with similar manufacturing methods in my previous position.

We had entered the fray just as production of Leyland's two most successful engines, the 0/680 and 0/400 series was at its peak. Both Tom and I were fortunate to have taken over a well-disciplined factory and the foremen who supervised the various lines and sections made our settling in period almost stress free. I say almost as there was one person we both dreaded ascending the stairs that led up to the large balcony office that we shared – the imposing figure of Jack Smith. Now Jack was the superintendent of the aforesaid engine assembly area and a more dedicated manager and nicer guy you could never hope to meet. So why then should his frequent visits cause our hearts to beat that little bit faster? Try as we might to reach the production targets set, there was always that elusive component part that Jack would require on the assembly line that we were in danger of not delivering on time.

It did not take long for us to learn that Jack was the eternal pessimist, a definite 'glass half empty' man and if he believed there was the slightest chance that a part would not be delivered on time then he felt duty bound to inform the potential perpetrators of what he considered an unforgivable crime akin to treason. Machine breakdowns, material shortages, manpower issues or any of the 101 other problems that could affect on time delivery were unacceptable reasons for failure in Jack's book. Any attempt to trot out such excuses would be met with his usual response of, "Well get it sorted; that's why they gave you the job in the first place." However, and despite the frequent visits, Jack's warnings did act as backup to our official progress system and we realized that he was seldom wrong in his ringing of the alarm bells – but just about a week or so to early.

Tom and I worked well together for a number of months until he was called to a higher office in the personnel department or to give it its posh new name, Human Resources. He was replaced by an old supervisory colleague, Tony Fishwick, one of the young foremen who had incurred the wrath of Wilf Hulme, and was one of the gang, along with myself and other miscreants, who had arrived back late to the Comet Shop after our delayed 'chippy' lunch a few years previous. There was also a change of Works Manager about this time when Alan Curtis took over the reins from Ken Bossonet. Alan was a true gentleman and a first class manager and I was sorry when he left the company to take up a senior post in the toiletry industry.

It wasn't long before Tony moved up the promotion ladder to be replaced by another of those reprobates who came back late from the 'chippy', a certain Mr Bob Jones. Now Bob was a great guy, full of fun and always smiling. He was very popular with all who knew him and he and I managed No 8 shop until engine manufacture ceased at the end of 1988. Bob was very enterprising and after leaving Leyland he set up his own garden maintenance business operating from his home in Burscough. It came as a great shock to all who knew him when just after his enterprise was beginning to thrive he passed away very suddenly.

As I mentioned earlier, our offices were situated on a balcony overlooking the workshop and Bob and I were looked after very well by young Margaret, an administration clerk who acted more like a secretary to us both. After some months operating from these offices, we got to recognize the footsteps of our more frequent visitors. Most were received with pleasure but the ones that always made us slightly apprehensive were, as mentioned earlier, those of Jack Smith chasing up some component part or other and those belonging to either Derek B or Colin F.

Now Derek and Colin were shop stewards with rather fearsome reputations (a reputation that only applied if you were part of the management team of course). Visits from either usually heralded a problem, either real or perceived and on hearing the slow determined plod of Derek's steps or the quicker lighter tread of Colin's often made me wish that there had been a backdoor in the office. In those early days, after a grilling from either one or t'other, I often felt that we were seen more as cruel overseers on a slave plantation rather than supervisors attempting to run a workshop.

But these were the early 1970's when any actions by the Leyland management were often viewed by the Trade Unions as highly suspicious and probably to the detriment of the workforce. Militancy at the Leyland plants was certainly not to the same level as it was in the car division although 'Red Robbo' had set the bar for others to follow and though there were a few hotheads who attempted to emulate their midland comrades, on the whole management and shop floor relationships were good. However, it took another decade before both sides began to operate as a real team.

As for Derek and Colin I probably hold them in greater esteem now than I did in those early days in No 8 Shop. Over the years I got to know them both very well and would go as far as to say in the final months leading to the demise of Leyland Engines, we became quite good friends. Derek sadly passed away a few years ago and as for Colin, an ex-miner from Wigan, well I'm not sure. I'd like to think he was still walking the streets of his hometown and enjoying a well-earned retirement.

Chapter 23 – And The Winner Is…

It was during my early years as the superintendent of No 8 Shop, a position that was later to receive the much grander title of Area Manager, that I came into contact with 'lucky' Frank Sowman, a foreman in the engine test area. Why lucky you may ask? Well the good fortune that Frank enjoyed was certainly not work related. It would be difficult to imagine a more intimidating environment in which to work than the area where Frank earned his money - the engine test shop. The noise of a dozen or so commercial vehicle engines undergoing rigorous test procedures was enough to shatter the eardrums of the unwary and to enter this area without wearing ear defenders was to guarantee hearing problems in later life.

No, Frank's luck came courtesy of the prolific returns from the many competitions that he entered. The 1970's and 80's were undoubtedly the golden age for competitions. You could hardy pick up a newspaper or magazine or enter a store without coming across the opportunity to win a car, a boat, a TV set or an all expenses paid cruise or holiday to some far off idyllic corner of the world – and Frank had won them all. Was I jealous? To darn tootin' I was! However, unlike others who considered that Frank's success was purely down to lady luck, I knew different.

Unlike the current crop of competitions that rely on entrants answering inane questions such as, 'What day follows Monday?" reducing the competition to nothing more than a lucky dip, in those days the budding competitor was required to have a little more about him. Most of the competitions, in the final analysis, required the would-be winners to come up with a snappy slogan such as; 'Complete the following sentence in 12 words or less – I always choose Boozers Beer because…' Now this is where Frank excelled and his apt and often amusing slogans had won him a bagful of prizes over the years.

Sitting next to him one day in the works canteen I asked him as to what did he attribute his success? "Sweat, toil and tears initially with a modicum of imagination and a pinch of inspiration at the end," was his response. After further prompting he informed me that if I wanted to try my hand at the competition game then the first absolute necessity was to subscribe to the 'Competitors' Journal', a monthly publication that contained news of all the competitions that were running at the time and tips about how to approach them. The next requirement was to decide which ones were worth entering and always to submit multi entries and of course the 'cruncher' was to come up with a catchy and memorable slogan that was appropriate to the product.

Thus armed, I made my first foray into the competition field – and won a holiday for two in Puerto Rico in the Caribbean! The ironic part of it was there was no slogan to compose but rather a matter of placing a number of bathing beauties in order of their attributes. However, having taken Frank's advice on board, I sent in enough entries to cover all permutations and obviously one of them had to be correct. It cost me a fortune in postage but the end result made it all worthwhile.

After this initial success there was no doubt that the competition bug had well and truly bitten me. From then on, most of my spare time was spent in gathering entry forms and filling them in and I had come up with a rather good slogan that I could adapt to cover most types of competitions (no! I'm not going to tell you what it was – who knows, this type of competition may return some day). Suffice it to say that my slogan appeared to appeal to the judges and for a period of about five years I never paid for a holiday, often enjoying at least two a year. My first computer was courtesy of a popular brand of soup and our first colour TV set came due a liking of a certain brand of meat paste (or so I told them).

I suppose the biggest win I had, thanks to a well known brand of batteries, was an all expenses trip to Spain for four people to see all the second stage matches, semi-finals and final of the 1982 world cup. We were based on Madrid's principal thoroughfare, a 6-lane highway known as the Grand Via in a rather ordinary hotel that went with the dubious name of The Rex. As well as seeing all the matches, including the final in the Bernabeu Stadium, we had a fantastic time exploring this magnificent city. Most of our memories of our time in Spain's capital city were happy ones – apart from the time when 95% of the residents of our hotel went down with 'Montezuma's Revenge' a day before the big semi-final in Seville.

The Rex - Our Hotel in Madrid

For some unknown reason, I was one of the lucky 5% who had escaped the sickness and the bus that had been chartered to ferry us to Seville that day was less than half full. I had been entrusted with the match tickets of all the guests who were to ill to travel the 330 miles between the two cities, with the strict instruction to sell them outside the ground for the best possible price. I replied that I would do my best.

It's strange isn't it when you know that there are toilets close to hand that the bowels in general behave themselves. However, when our guide announced that we were about to pass through the Toledo Mountains and that there would be no toilet facilities for the next 10 miles or so, the human pipeline takes this news as a sign to go out of kilter. I suppose we were about 4 miles into the 'no bogs' zone when the first urge hit me. A couple of miles further along the mountainous road, both sphincter muscles now working to the limit of their capabilities and just about holding their own and with beads of sweat now adorning my forehead, I looked out of the window with the forlorn hope of finding a lay-by were perhaps the coach could stop – unfortunately all I saw was a rock face to one side and a sheer drop on the other.

The fact that I eventually made it to the little roadside café bar unsoiled was something of a miracle. I dashed into the dimly lit interior and enquired of the startled bartender, " Servicios senor por favor?" He pointed vaguely to the rear of his rather seedy premises to which I hastened and tugged open the door – to find myself in a small field with a ramshackle and rusty corrugated iron construction in the centre. It was probably the most ugly and nastiest appointed toilet that I had ever come across but at that moment it seemed like a palace set in an oasis. The door was nothing more than a section of the corrugated iron sheeting that I quickly moved to one side – and in doing so promptly released, what I thought at the time was the total fly population of Spain. Under normal circumstances I would have fled the scene, but my need was now overpowering.

As my eyes became accustomed to the dim interior I noticed that a large pit had been crudely dug in the centre of the plot with what appeared to be crude footholds at each side. From the tin roof dangled a rope and it quickly became apparent to me as to how these various trappings were to be used. Suitably unadorned, I grabbed the rope, braced myself in the footholds and – well I reckon you can guess the rest.

The feeling of blessed relief was overpowering, but now that the cause of my erstwhile distress had been removed I was able to take stock of exactly where I was. Clinging to a badly frayed rope, dangling over an indescribable pit that was god knows how deep with my feet slowly slipping out of the rudely constructed footholds.

I quickly regained my composure and terra firma and after adjusting my dress, I hurried out of the veritable hellhole, leaving it once more to the swarms of flies and other unspeakable creatures that were now reclaiming their unsavoury kingdom.

As I finally emerged into the bright sunshine, it was not surprising to see that a little queue had formed outside, waiting patiently to use the rudimentary facility. Many made it to the rudely fashioned door but as far as I could ascertain, few if any actually passed across the threshold. For the remainder of the journey to Seville there was much whispering and fingers pointed in my general direction and I believe that I was held in awe and grudging admiration as the daring but foolhardy 'Brit' that bravely battled and beat the sh*t…

We arrived in Seville just a couple of hours or so before the start of the match and after a hastily consumed sandwich and a further visit to a rather more salubrious toilet, I hurried to the concourse outside the magnificent stadium to sell the tickets that had been entrusted to me. This particular semi-final was between France and Germany and I thought I would have little problem in offloading the tickets – how wrong could I have been? With less than half-an-hour before kick-off I realized that there was probably more ticket touts than fans on that vast concourse and very few tickets appeared to be changing hands.

A voice with a distinct cockney accent whispered in my ear, "How many you got son?" I told him the number I had been entrusted with and with a shake of his head he informed me that I had as much chance of selling them as England had of winning the cup. As they had already been eliminated this of course meant – no chance! "Tell you what son," he said glancing at my tickets, "They're pretty lousy seats. I've got probably the best in the house, next to the royal box they are and I can't shift 'em. Tell you what, I'll give you two of my seats for that little lot of yours – deal?" Time was now pressing and kick-off was imminent. Realizing that the tickets would be worthless after the match I agreed to his offer.

The guy had been as good as his word. The tickets indeed were within touching distance of the royal box and when Juan Carlos eventually arrived late, delaying the kick-off by about twenty minutes, I'm sure he directed a smile of apology towards my seat – or then again it was probably just my imagination.

It turned out to be a cracker of a match with Germany winning, undeservedly I thought, on penalties after extra time. After a long, tiring but uneventful journey home I then had to face the wrath of all those disappointed people who had given me their tickets to sell. Fortunately they understood the dilemma I had been faced with and were very forgiving, even to the point of applauding my audacity at exchanging their tickets for a seat next to the king of Spain…

France v Germany in the 1982 World Cup semi-final

Safely back home in the UK I continued entering virtually every competition that presented itself and the winning streak continued. However, the competitors 'Holy Grail', a car, eluded all my finest efforts but it would have been churlish to complain. From then on, Frank and I were considered to be a pair of 'lucky bu****s' and to echo Frank's response to such taunts, 'Ye! And the more competitions I enter the luckier I seem to get.' It was a sad day for both of us when this type of competition went out of fashion and from then on I sadly had to pay for my own holidays.

Chapter 24 – The 'A' Team

The Real A-Team

The Pretenders

As well as keeping the wheels of industry turning, the plant continued to attract its share of visiting dignitaries. When such visits were imminent it was the usual practice to 'blitz' the factory with cleaning teams about a week or so beforehand to ensure that the visitors would be suitably impressed by our attention to housekeeping. However, no matter how much effort was applied there always appeared to be a 'grot spot' that did not escape the eagle eye of the then factory manager Bob Bullen and further shifting, re-stacking, scraping and brushing was required to meet with his exacting standards. His final nod of approval was always followed by the statement, "Now why can't you keep it like this at all times?"

Of course Bob was right but no matter how hard we tried to achieve this permanent state of cleanliness it always appeared to elude us? It took Denis Chapman, one of our general labourers to point out where we were going wrong. By tradition, each line or section had its own team of labourers and their duties were to keep their particular area of responsibility clean and tidy and to be fair they were pretty good at the task.

Denis however brought to management attention that this set up was overly territorial and created pockets or areas that no one appeared to have direct responsibility for. He suggested that a dedicated team of labourers be set up to tackle the issue. I agreed that it was worth a try and as he had come up with idea I asked him to select two other labourers and head the 'grime busters' team for a trial period.

It was an unqualified success and soon earned the guys responsible the impressive title of the A-Team. Dennis, Trevor Baxter with a third member whose name escapes me proved to be just what the plant had been crying out for these many years. No longer where the pre dignitary visits by Bob Bullen tinged with the apprehension of him finding fault with the factory housekeeping – it was now always immaculate, thanks to our own Mr T, Denis Chapman and his intrepid team.

Their services were always in great demand and the team remained active right up to the date of Leyland Engine's sad demise. The reason I have included this little story in my memoirs is to show that not all great concepts come from the top and why it is so important to listen to the thoughts and ideas from others, no matter what position they hold or where they are placed in the factory hierarchy.

Chapter 25 – The Times They are A-Changing

The next few years were pretty uneventful for those of us directly involved with production. Although we were aware that the political aspect of the business was becoming 'interesting', our efforts continued to centre around maintaining a smile on Jack Smith's face by keeping the engine assembly lines running, content to leave the politics of the business to others more qualified.

However, even us non-political types could not fail to be anything other than concerned when in 1981 the Truck & Bus Division was split and each would henceforth operate as autonomous companies. I have always believed that in unity there is strength and that this division would do little to ensure the continuance of either company as trading conditions got tougher.

Despite the fact that engine orders were pretty steady, there were some worrying trends, particularly with reject levels and material shortages. The original Plant

Operating Procedures had been brought up to date, an exercise in which I was heavily involved, the old piecework structure was replaced by a system that evened out potential earnings across the various factories and the 100% final inspection of components by an independent inspection team had made way for a system where the onus for checking work produced devolved to the operator.

Unfortunately all these initiatives failed to induce a meaningful reduction in the level of rejects, but thanks to stringent testing procedures of the final product our customers did not suffer as all non-conforming engines or parts were identified and contained within the plant. However, these unacceptable quality failures were costing the company needless expense in a market that was becoming extremely competitive. Something needed to happen to halt this worrying trend – and it did.

Chapter 26 – To the Manor Borne

Leyland Motors as a company was always very quality conscious, a feature which I believe reflected in the excellence of the final product as it was presented to the customer. However, and as I touched on in the previous chapter, this was not always reflected in the various manufacturing processes and over the years much time and money was wasted in producing components that did not meet specification. It was something of a standing joke in the company that whenever the lodge pool on the Farington site was periodically drained, it was found to contain enough scrap component parts to manufacture a fleet of commercial vehicles. When competition was much less cutthroat, these losses could be absorbed, as profit margins were set high enough to cover them. As the SCANIAS VOLVOS and DAFS of the industry began to make inroads in what for decades had been traditional Leyland markets, something needed to be done. Somehow the company had to master the art of sustained quality production, not only with the final product but also with all the manufacturing processes that led up to it.

A number of quality initiatives had been set up in earlier years consisting of short duration courses and seminars, which I believe had little or no impact on the majority of employees who undertook them. The widely held view was to attend, listen carefully, fill in the questionnaire and then go back to the coalface and carry on as before. It took the arrival of new quality director to alter this mindset. The first major discipline to be introduced in the early 1980's centred not directly on quality issues but rather the way that the business was conducted. It was an externally based course that carried the imposing title of 'Managing For Results' or MFR as it was more familiarly known as.

The MFR was a residential course held at the Rover Staff College, which is situated in Haseley Manor, a beautiful old manor house situated in its own extensive grounds in rural Warwickshire. The course was run over four separate weekly sessions and was attended not only by Leyland employees but also included a cross-section of people from Leyland subsidiaries and other Rover based companies. The MFR programme was initially introduced in 1980 and it came about due to a much-needed change in Management style. The Rover group of companies wanted its managers to 'manage by objectives' rather than by the old and outmoded way of 'reactive' management or as it was more informally known 'by the seat of your pants!'

In was in 1983 when Dougie Gornall and I were selected to attend the course as the representatives of the now separate companies, Leyland Trucks by me and Leyland Buses by him. Dougie, like myself, was an Area Manager and also a very good friend of long standing. This was just as well when we found that we were billeted together in the same bedroom. Despite this firm friendship I was however somewhat relieved to find that we had at least been allocated separate beds.

We had been briefed as to the contents of the course and it did appear initially that it had all the makings of a long hard slog. It also required the participants to make personal presentations, which is an element of business seminars that most people, even seasoned managers, dread. However, we were in for a pleasant surprise, as it transpired that the course tutor, Dave Davies, a 'Scouser' far from home, was not only brilliant at making what could have been a dull course interesting but had also been blessed with a sense of humour that seems to characterize so many of his compatriots that hail from the banks of the Mersey. Every lesson was made that much more interesting by Dave's unique teaching style. Despite the serious content he was charged to deliver, his somewhat informal and light-hearted approach never failed to grip and hold the undivided attention of the class. Even the dreaded presentations were received and delivered without the presence of the fear factor, which leads to a very interesting and personal aside.

I had worked hard preparing my presentation and was very pleased by the reception I received from Dave and my fellow presenters on its delivery. The following day I was informed that there was likely to be a vacancy in the tutorial staff and would I be interested in applying for the position. It appeared that my presentation had attracted the attention of more than just my colleagues and the college believed that I had the makings of a reasonably capable tutor. I of course was flattered and must admit the thought of tutoring as a full-time career did have some appeal.

My Pencil sketch of Haseley Manor - 1984

After an informal chat with the college principal, he advised me to give it some thought. He also suggested that I should actually run a session on my next visit so that I would have hands-on experience as to what the position entailed. This I did and although nervous at first I grew in confidence as the session continued. Apparently I had done OK and was asked if I would like to be considered for a teaching position at the college. Of course this was not a decision I could take unilaterally. I had a wife and family to consider and as the job would require me to relocate to the midlands, would such a move be attractive for my family?

After much soul-searching and hours of dialogue with family, friends and my current employers I decided that the move was not for me. The tipping point had been an indication from the Leyland Plant Director that if the course were to be adopted and run as an in-house seminar at Leyland then I would have every chance of being part of the tutorial team. It was with some sorrow that I informed the college head of my decision. However, he was understanding of my situation and indicated that if I ever had a change of heart he was only a phone-call away.

So then, back to the nitty-gritty of the course. Being residential it was not all spent working and the fact that Haseley Manor was blest with a well stocked bar and a convivial host and hostess, there were many happy hours spent carousing with colleagues. Despite the fact that all group members got on well together there was a certain amount of friendly rivalry apparent. We were split fairly evenly between long-in-the-tooth managers and fast rising stars and it was inevitable that sooner or later some sort of challenge would be issued – and it was. It was to be in the form of a general knowledge quiz with our tutor Dave acting as quizmaster. Dougie and I formed part of the 'golden oldies' team and the fun began when the 'opposition' turned up wearing short trousers and dunces' caps. The latter turned out to be quite fitting as the 'old grey hairs' thrashed them completely.

The old grey hairs emerge triumphant

Fitting attire for the losers

The weekly courses progressed over about a six-months period and I think I can speak assuredly for all the attendees when I say that not only was it a thoroughly enjoyable experience but that we also returned to our various companies as much better equipped managers. At Leyland this was the first part of the trilogy of disciplines that would hopefully equip us to compete on an equal footing in the commercial vehicle market with our European competitors.

They'll miss Dougie at Haseley Manor

Chapter 27 – Back to the Coal Face

And so flushed with all the good stuff we had gathered up at Hasely Manor, Dougie and I returned to our respective bases keen and ready to implement at least some of the ideas. However, we were first tasked by Les Southworth to make a formal presentation to the company directors and members of senior management. Now if

142

you had asked me to undertake such a task prior to our attendance of the MFR course in the presence of such an eminent audience, I think I would have run a mile. But our loins had been well and truly girded thanks to our tutor Dave Davies and the many presentations we had made over the duration of the course made the prospect far less daunting.

Presentation day dawned and Dougie and I were aware that as well as having supporters in the audience, there were also those who had yet to be convinced of the benefits of introducing the concept of MFR across the Leyland plants. During and after the presentation there were many hard and searching questions asked but despite the grilling we received I think that we convinced the majority of attendees that the concept was worth introducing across both the truck and bus plants.

Dougie and I then sat down with our respective plant directors to discuss the best way forward. At this time we were still in the frame for fronting MFR and despite the fact that I think I would have enjoyed the challenge, it soon became obvious that this would be impractical. We were informed in no uncertain terms that taking on the task would be as well as continuing with our other management duties. After further discussion we managed to convince the directors that to do justice to both disciplines, magic wands would be required and as J K Rowling had not yet created Ollivanders in Diagon Alley, there was little chance of obtaining even a small one. It was therefore proposed that tutors for MFR would be outsourced.

Having now been relieved of our training duties we could now concentrate on introducing some of the aspects of the MFR concept. The discipline that appealed to me most was the introduction of logbooks for the shop foremen. They appeared to me to serve a number of useful purposes and would certainly make supervisors more aware of their responsibilities and give managers a greater opportunity to assess the performances achieved by their subordinates and to implement any corrective actions that may have been necessary.

It turned out to be a more involved exercise than initially visualized. For starters I was responsible for 13 foremen at this time and with each individual I had to draw up a multi point plan of action. These factors included agreeing job requirements and targets; comparing performance with targets; Identifying the cause of missed targets; agreeing corrective actions; agreeing new targets and finally agreeing a personal development plan. This was no mean task multiplied by 13 and took up a big slice of my management time initially. However, I considered it time well spent and I believe that these log books played a significant part in improving the operating procedures of the factory…

As no doubt you will already have gathered from previous chapters, there was always time for workmates and colleagues to get together socially. As well as the sporting competitions and cabarets, a certain specialist group of men in No 8 shop had a rather unique way of getting their members away from work issues and banding together for financial and social purposes that were to have mutual benefits for all participants.

Now David Taylor was an engine assembly foreman and also a very astute businessman. He was a chap who as well as owning a number of residential properties in Preston was also a keen and quite successful dabbler in the stock market. It was no surprise therefore that many of his fellow foremen regularly sought his advice on which stocks to follow and which to avoid. Now being a true entrepreneur and a good-hearted Lancashire lad to boot, he suggested that all the Spurrier Works foremen who were so inclined should start an investment club.

The idea really caught the imagination of the foremen and an investment club was duly formed and was christened with the rather obvious name of the 'Blue Collar Club'. Under the guidance of Dave assisted by fellow foreman Jimmy Guy, a set of simple rules were drawn up and very soon the club was up and running. I first learned of the club when Dave and Jimmy approached me to ask if I would allow Margaret, our admin' clerk to act as secretary for the club. I told them 'yes' on one condition, that I would be allowed to join the ranks. After due consideration and the fact that I had until recently been a foreman, I was granted the privilege.

Just how did it operate you might ask? Well share allocations in the club were offered at a payment of £5 per month per share, with a maximum of 4 shares per member. At regular intervals, meetings were held in the upstairs lounge of the LMSAC. Members were invited to submit the name of a company that they considered worth investing in. Long discussions then took place in an effort to whittle the suggestions down to one or perhaps two and the accrued cash from member's contributions were then allocated in purchasing the shares chosen. When the serious side of the business was concluded, the rest of the evenings were spent enjoying each other's company and I suppose it was inevitable that there was sometimes the odd disagreement.

The one that springs to mind most readily was when Joe, an unprepared young foreman happened to mention that the chicken he had eaten for his tea that night was so tough it must have been an old 'broiler'. Within minutes the lounge was in uproar; half the assembly in favour of a broiler being an old bird and the rest that it was indeed a young fowl. So intense did the argument become that I as a manager, and therefore considered neutral, was tasked with finding out the truth. Unfortunately there was no 'Google' or 'Ask Jeeves' around at the time and so I wrote to the one authority that would hopefully be able to settle the dispute, namely the British Poultry Council. A week or so later a 3-page reply (with photos attached) was received and the mystery was solved. It turned out that a broiler was indeed a young chicken. Joe had in fact dined on a 'boiler' that fateful night and hadn't realized what a furore he would cause by confusing the two. I think he regrets opening his mouth to this day.

As the Blue Collar Club grew in popularity, it extended its remit not to just making stock market investments but to include social trips out for the members. The most memorable of these was a weekend away in the Lincolnshire village of Woodhall Spa, famous for being the wartime base of the famed 617 RAF squadron, or to give it its more popular name – The Dambusters. We stayed in the Petwood Hotel, which had been the actual base for Barnes Wallis, Guy Gibson and the rest of the brave airmen that carried out the famous 'bouncing bomb' raid on the Ruhr Valley dams.

The one outstanding feature of the hotel was the 20ft length of pine tree mounted over the fireplace in one of the comfortable lounges in the hotel. Apparently this treetop had actually crashed through the cockpit of one of the Lancaster bombers that took part in the memorable low-level raid. We listened in awe as the barman told us this fascinating story and I recall someone saying that we should raise our glasses and toast the brave airmen whose brave and heroic actions had undoubtedly shortened the war. Guy Gibson was of course not present to witness this but then again we had our own 'Guy' and little persuasion was necessary for our own Jimmy Guy, an ex RAF man himself, to rise (somewhat unsteadily) and propose one of the most heart-rending and memorable toasts that I have ever heard – Ah these were indeed happy days.

Despite the selection of the odd 'turkey' or two, most of the investment choices made by the BCC proved to be financially sound. All the members looked forward to the annual payout, which usually coincided with the two-week summer holiday and more often than not resulted in either an upgrade of destination or more cash to spend – or both. It was a sad day when the club finally disbanded but I'm sure that every member would agree that it had been a great experience, both financially and socially…

Despite a slowly improving situation with both quality and productivity issues, the diminishing order book was becoming a concern. It was inevitable that in the face of growing competition that there would be a number of manpower reductions. Of all the tasks that faced me as a member of the management team there is no doubt that my necessary involvement in such negative activity was the one I detested most. When you have worked with a group of people for weeks, months and even years it is no easy assignment to have to inform them that their skills or presence in the factory is no longer required.

I always attempted to communicate this sad news to each recipient with understanding and sympathy and although it had never been company practice to write individual references, I personally believed that this was the least we could do for good people who were loosing their livelihood through no fault of their own. So if anyone reading this book wishes to take me to task for ignoring this particular company policy, well now's your chance as I must have written many a dozen and it always left me with a sense of deep satisfaction when I learned of ex-employees who had found work, perhaps even as a result of a reference that I had written.

On the whole most individuals received redundancy notice with good grace. There were unfortunately a few exceptions when individuals took the news as a personal attack by me on their abilities. To a degree I realized that these outbursts stemmed from disappointment and anger and that I as the deliverer of the bad news was their natural target to relieve themselves of the frustration. There were a couple of occasions when I thought that the frustration might have escalated to physical violence but thankfully this was never the case…

Chapter 28 – Crosby to the Rescue

No – Not this one.

This one!

Despite becoming much leaner our competitiveness in the commercial vehicle market place showed little if any improvement. Process and manufacturing quality remained a burgeoning issue and needed to be addressed if the company were to have any prospects of surviving. Something new, innovative and workable had to be found, and quickly, to address the current situation. Well they do say that cometh the moment then cometh the man and in Leyland's case that man turned out to be Philip Crosby.

Philip Crosby was an American quality engineer whose sincere manufacturing belief was to 'Do It Right First Time'. This philosophy had been successfully adopted by a number of companies and so our Quality Director at this time, John Jones, decided that it should be introduced as our saving grace at Leyland Trucks. The four underlying principles of the concept were remarkably simple but had obviously been highly successful when applied as a total concept. They were as follows: -

1. The definition of quality is conformance to the product and customer requirements.

2. The system of quality is prevention.

3. The performance standard is zero defects relative to requirements.

4. The measurement of quality is the price of non-conformance.

Crosby not only believed but also proved that any organization that established a quality programme based on these absolutes would see savings returns that would more than pay off the cost of the programme, hence his now world famous motto 'Quality is Free'.

Now wake up at the back there! Yes I realize that all this technical stuff can be somewhat sleep inducing but I believe it is important to set out the Crosby principles in order for you to see how these were interpreted and utilized so successfully at Leyland Trucks and later at Leyland Engines. To me the Crosby concept was successful because it involved everybody who worked for the company. Previous attempts to introduce whichever quality courses were doing the rounds at that time either failed or had only limited success because of the fundamental failing of not including the total workforce. It was always considered enough to send managers and senior supervisors on these 'flavour of the month' courses, yet no matter how inspired or fired up they might have been on their return to the plant, they found it nigh on impossible to introduce new quality thinking simply because the total workforce had not been involved from the outset. The 'us' and 'them' mentality still held sway and anything that went against time-honoured ways of doing things was more often than not treated with suspicion. Thankfully the Crosby philosophy eliminated these deep set and negative traditions as everyone from the highest paid director to the lowliest tea boy were included.

So how do you set about educating a total workforce? No doubt there is a common thread but surely there will be differing requirements for the different classes of employees? It was achieved by what I would best describe as a 'trickle down' system. Senior managers attended the executive college which was an exhaustive course held externally. Middle managers attended a similar external college called the 'Quality Improvement Process' or QIP course. All supervisors undertook a 'Quality Education System' that was conducted by managers who had taken the QIP course after additional training by Philip Crosby personnel. Finally, all other employees (including that humble tea boy) attended the 'Quality Awareness Experience', which in turn was conducted by supervisors who had successfully completed the 'QES' course.

Leyland Management Team attend a Crosby Quality Course

When all employees had been introduced and educated into the Crosby quality teachings, it was then time to turn classroom teaching into practical, realistic and hands on processes. The quality improvements sought by the company could never hope to be achieved overnight and it was important to remember that the concept was to be viewed as a journey rather than a destination.

Bearing in mind at all times the philosophy of the 4 absolutes; it was first necessary to take stock of our current quality position by measuring and charting our non-conformances. This achieved it was now necessary to aim towards eliminating them by setting up Corrective Action Teams (CATS) to begin the journey by first reducing the non-conformances by short term fixes, with the ultimate objective of eliminating them through longer term correction plans.

It was still necessary to have some form of structural hierarchy when setting up these teams to ensure that the quality issues causing the most pain were tackled initially. A steering committee was first set up comprising company executives and senior managers. The next level of control was called the Quality Improvement Team (QIT) and comprised of at least one executive member and would include representatives from all sections of the business with the majority drawn from graduates of the QIP college. From this body would then come the master plan that required the formation of lower level teams (CATS) to look at particular quality issues. Each team elected a co-ordinator, which linked horizontally and vertically with other teams. The overriding aim of all these teams was to achieve 'zero defects'.

To achieve what was once considered the unachievable required commitment from all classes. However it was considered most important that without visible commitment from the top and not just lip service, the concept would quickly fall into disrepute. This act of obligation was achieved through executives and senior managers not only sitting in the top tier teams but by also taking their place in the grass roots teams. The ultimate aim was for the philosophy not to be considered as the Crosby concept of quality achievement but rather to become the 'norm' and second nature to everybody.

Did the concept have the desired effect? The first encouraging signs that made me believe that the company was onto something rather special was the way that certain employees engaged in the philosophy. As in all large companies we had our share of detractors who appeared to take delight in finding fault with any new management initiatives. I harboured fears that this would be the case with the Crosby concept. I'm happy to report that my fears were unfounded. The fact that they had been personally involved and not had new ideas merely thrust upon them changed all the previous negative energy into something decidedly positive. No longer did I dread those well-known footsteps approaching the office door that usually heralded such opening phrases as, "My members are not happy with…" Such meetings now were more on the lines of, "Me and the lads have been looking at such-and such a problem and have come up with some ideas." With attitudes like this it was nigh on impossible not to at least improve the situation.

Leyland Engines Management Team - 1987

So what did the company finally achieve? By now our little empire at Spurrier works had been divorced from Leyland Trucks (more of this in a later chapter) and was now simply Leyland Engines. Although the company was destined to be consigned to the commercial vehicle history books, in the last months of manufacture and operating with 50% temporary employees, we achieved zero defects status on final engine audit. This from a pre-Crosby situation of an average of 23 defects per engine was a remarkable achievement that was never truly recognised due to the eventual plant closure.

Proud members of the engine production team who helped achieve

'Zero Defects'

Chapter 29 – MRP II – We Need You

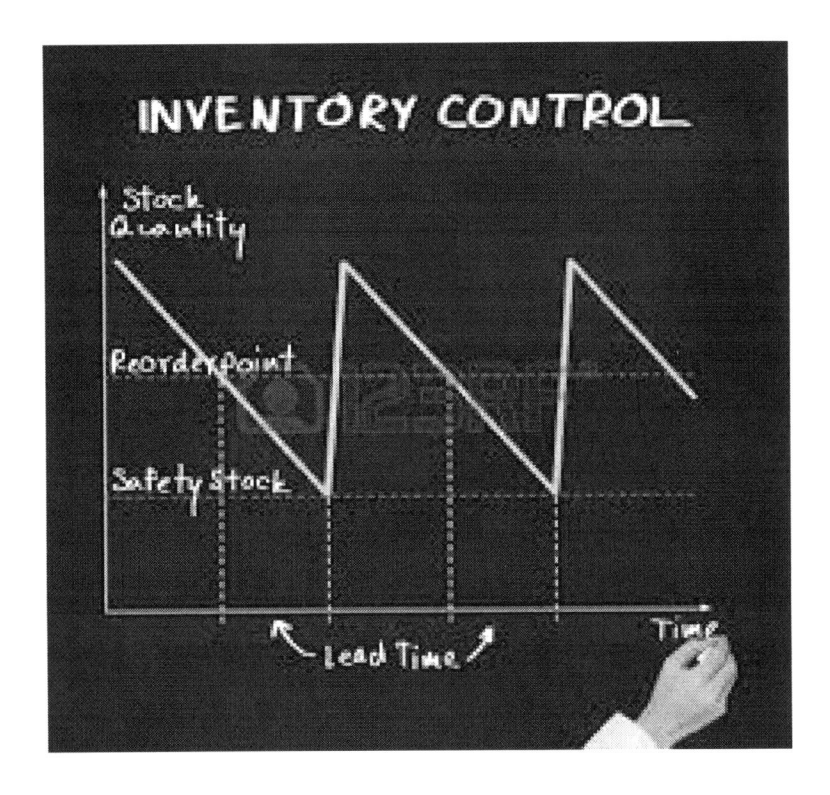

The quality issues now well on the way to being resolved, the next most pressing problem was on-time procurement of materials. Of course there were systems of a sort in place that worked reasonably well, thanks in the main to a team of procurement people such as Randy Lister and Roger Metcalf who had been around long enough to know all the tricks of the trade. Yet despite their best efforts, which often resulted in parts being only a day late rather than a week, it still resulted in interruptions to the manufacturing programme. I well remember a high-level procurement meeting when a vital part coming from Switzerland was, according to Randy, likely to be late due to an avalanche that had blocked off the Simplon Tunnel. Our Op's Director at the time fixed him with a baleful look and suggested that he get himself a shovel and go help to clear it. Quick as a flash Randy replied he would love to but unfortunately shovels were also on shortage. Of course Randy's riposte brought the house down but also highlighted how exposed we were in not getting our materials in on time. Like the problem with quality something needed to be done – and it was – welcome to MRPII.

MRPII or Manufacturing Resource Planning was the natural successor to MRP or Materials Resource Planning and was the brainchild of American industrialist, Ollie Wight. Now while the latter concentrates purely on obtaining materials, the former, thanks to Ollie's vision, embraced all aspects of manufacturing and is defined as a method for the effective planning of all resources of a manufacturing company. It is a system that is ideally computer based with software developed for the particular business of the company. It comprises a number of modules that include such disciplines as

1. Master production schedule (MPS)

2. Item master data (technical data)

3. Bill of materials (BOM) (technical data)

4. Production resources data (manufacturing technical data)

5. Inventories and orders (inventory control)

6. Purchasing management

7. Material requirements planning (MRP)

8. Shop floor control (SFC)

9. Capacity planning or capacity requirements planning (CRP)

10. Standard costing (cost control)

11. Cost reporting / management (cost control)

OK, so maybe I'm boring some of you rigid once again with all this data, but then again I suppose there will always be those among you who relish such detail. For those of you less pedantic readers who prefer a picture to words, here is a chart that summarises all the various modules very well.

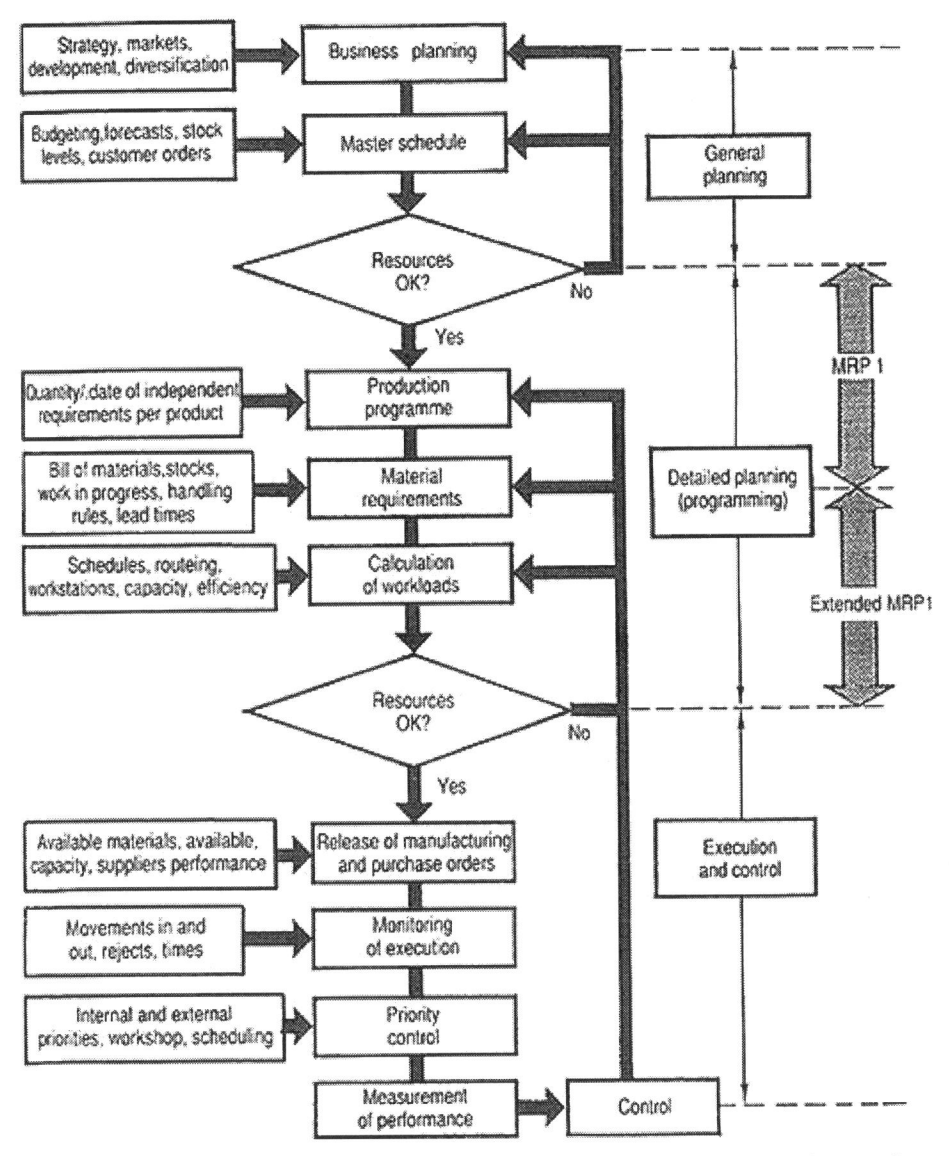

Around 1980, over-frequent changes in sales forecasts, entailing continual reajustments in production, as well as the unsuitability of the parameters fixed buy the system, led MRP (Material Requirement Planning) to evolve into a new concept : Manufacturating Resource Planning or MRP2

Chart produced by kind permission of the author, Jean-Babtiste Waldner.

All of these modules were introduced into the factory and all the personnel that would be required to operate the various disciplines were sent on appropriate courses. However there were still those that believed that this was just another flash in the pan system that in the end would never resolve the problems we had endured for years, that of having an unacceptable high inventory of some materials and acute shortages of others. One such non-believer had the temerity to compose and post on the main factory notice board the following ditty.

<u>Battle Hymn of The Purchasing Department</u>

Oh we are the MRP army

On shortages we've declared war

To the cause we are all dedicated

We'll not cease 'til the battle is o'er

To the front our big guns we have mustered

From restraints we will knock seven bells

So forward men this is the moment

But please tell me whose ordered the shells?

Yes we are the MRP army

The decisions we make sure take guts

With Messrs Hastie and Metcalf our colonels

The rest of the troop just plain nuts

But now we're convinced that we've cracked it

Right now we're descending the hill

Next month we are sure to hit programme

For at last they've reduced it to nil

And when the last trump it has sounded

From that great MRP in the sky

When we all meet the grand 'Master Scheduler'

Who will announce to us all with a sigh

Harps and halos are promised tomorrow

There's no doubt that we're in quite a stew

Ollie Wight has converted the 'Gaffer'

Now Heaven's running on MRPII

Anon

Despite the undoubted poetic charm of this odd ode, its rather negative message turned out to be just that – negative. Like all new systems there were teething problems but eventually we bade a not so fond farewell to material shortages and even had the honour of Ollie Wight presenting Peter Matheson, our Op's Director, with our certificate which proclaimed that Leyland Engines was now an accepted MRPII company. I cannot honestly say that there were never any more material shortages but they were now rare occurrences and in most cases, because of the total MRP II structure, we were better able to predict a potential shortage and modify the manufacturing programme to suit the materials that were available.

Chapter 30 – The Show Goes On

KEEP CALM THE SHOW MUST GO ON

I think the time is right for me to bring you up to speed with all that happened during my last few years at Leyland. I have already mentioned the parting of the ways between the Truck and Bus divisions in 1981 and in 1986 Leyland DAF was formed following the take over of the truck division by DAF, the Dutch commercial vehicle manufacturers. This resulted in a further sub-division of the business when Leyland Engines was formed as a separate entity to Leyland Trucks. The whole takeover was viewed by some as a lifeline for Leyland whilst others more pragmatic viewed it more as the thin edge of the wedge, allowing DAF an easy route into Leyland's traditional markets and who would be discarded when this had been achieved.

There was still those however that saw an amusing side to this takeover and within days of the announcement the following 'proclamation' was found pinned to a number of notice boards. Even in the face of potential adversity Lancashire humour could not be repressed.

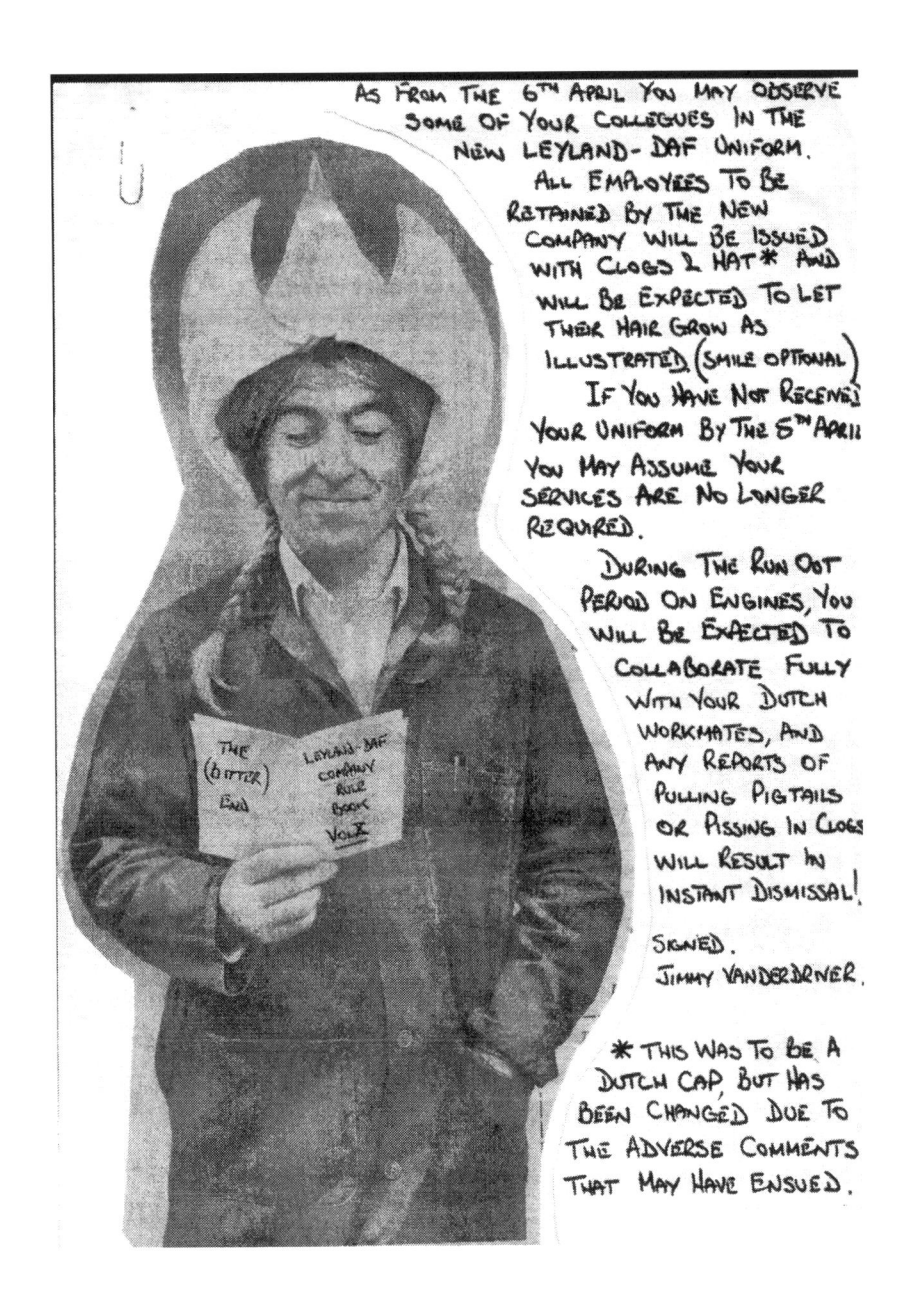

> AS FROM THE 6TH APRIL YOU MAY OBSERVE SOME OF YOUR COLLEAGUES IN THE NEW LEYLAND-DAF UNIFORM. ALL EMPLOYEES TO BE RETAINED BY THE NEW COMPANY WILL BE ISSUED WITH CLOGS & HAT* AND WILL BE EXPECTED TO LET THEIR HAIR GROW AS ILLUSTRATED. (SMILE OPTIONAL)
> IF YOU HAVE NOT RECEIVED YOUR UNIFORM BY THE 5TH APRIL YOU MAY ASSUME YOUR SERVICES ARE NO LONGER REQUIRED.
> DURING THE RUN OUT PERIOD ON ENGINES, YOU WILL BE EXPECTED TO COLLABORATE FULLY WITH YOUR DUTCH WORKMATES, AND ANY REPORTS OF PULLING PIGTAILS OR PISSING IN CLOGS WILL RESULT IN INSTANT DISMISSAL!
> SIGNED.
> JIMMY VANDERDRIVER.
>
> * THIS WAS TO BE A DUTCH CAP, BUT HAS BEEN CHANGED DUE TO THE ADVERSE COMMENTS THAT MAY HAVE ENSUED.

(Book held: "THE (bitter) END" / "LEYLAND-DAF COMPANY RULE BOOK Vol.I")

On the surface very little appeared to have changed apart from there now being a slimmer and more productive workforce that began at last to reap the rewards of the MFR, Crosby and MRPII initiatives.

It was in January 1987 that we learned that Leyland Bus had been sold to a consortium of management and banks. A purchase that probably proved lucrative for some but did little to improve the situation of the company. By the end of 1987 the directors were having doubts about the future of Leyland Bus and it came as no surprise when it was announced, in March 1988, that it had been sold to Volvo of Sweden.

During these concluding years, many initiatives were set up that complimented in the main, the Crosby quality philosophy. A number of successful CATS teams had been established and the defect rate in all areas was reducing fast. In order to keep the concept alive and fresh, competition was introduced across the plant. One of these initiatives came in the form of a splendid conformance shield that was awarded monthly to the department, office or section that had made the biggest contribution in eliminating defects or improving their efficiency. It became a keenly contested campaign with the monthly winners proudly displaying the shield in their area.

LATEST CONFORMANCE SHIELD AWARDS

ENGINES GET IT RIGHT! - "When you can measure what you are speaking about and express it in numbers, you know something about it". - Lord Kelvin -

Production Control:

Improving Programme Mix from 87.5% in August 1986 to 97% by March 1988.

Machine Shop Supervisors & Planners:

Achieving orders to finish dates for 4 conscutive weeks.

Heat Treatment Personnel:

For reducing Re-heats from 22% in 1987 to Zero for 3 consecutive weeks in April/May 1988.

Engine Assembly:

For achieving Zero defects on 4 measured areas in Engine Build Sequence in the same week?
Zero Defects - Pre-Test Audit
" - Cold Pressure Test
" - Bus Plant Audit
" - Sick Bay

There were also individual awards in the shape of 'zero defect mugs', cake presentations and shopping vouchers to be gained and like the shield, all these awards were keenly contested.

Just one of the rewards for achieving ZERO defects!

Leyland Engines had also started publishing an in-house newsletter that made it the ideal media for reporting on the various awards and each edition was eagerly awaited. The newsletter had initially been edited by Steve Maslaczyk from the Personnel Department and on his transfer he handed over the reins to his colleague Jock Gallagher who promptly hired me to act as his assistant scribe and photographer. I think it was the composing of various articles for the newsletter that awakened the passion in me for creative writing. Who knows, without that opportunity this book may never have been written (did I hear cries of mores the pity).

Leyland Engines NEWSLETTER

DECEMBER 1988 **ISSUE 24**

Season's Greetings

Who said there's no Father Christmas! He's alive and kicking, visited Engines recently, and shared in the Festivities in Spurrier Canteen.

We hope the festivities last into the Christmas period and wish you Good Luck, Good Health and Happiness through 1989.

The last ever Leyland Engines newsletter

It is something of a paradox but as Leyland engines became leaner, fitter, and more productive and had achieved zero defects in many departments over sustained periods, the requirement for its product lessened. I think most people in the commercial vehicle game realized that its two major products, the 0/400 and 0/680 series engines were coming to the end of a long and illustrious life. Potential replacements such as the 0/500 series and the AEC V8 had not lived up to expectations. In hindsight one could argue that if more of the profits gained in the 1960's and 70's had been directed towards commercial engine development rather than to the avaricious car plants then it could have been a totally different story. However it's easy to be wise with the benefit of hindsight and who am I to say that decisions taken then could have been more judicious.

So, here we were, trying to compete with the 'big boys' of Europe, including our on-site 'rivals', DAF, who of course manufactured their own range of engines in Holland. As the market became more squeezed, it did not take a genius to predict that if an engine plant had to be sacrificed in the face of such fierce competition it would not be the DAF factory where the axe would fall – and the worst fears of all the workforce were soon to be realized – Leyland Engines would cease to exist by the end of 1988.

Chapter 31 – Shocking News

The whole factory was devastated when the closure announcement was made. It had been somewhat expected during the previous few months yet when the news was finally delivered it was still hard to imagine that decades of engine manufacture would be over at Leyland in just a few short months.

The one saving grace was that the closure was not to be immediate. There were outstanding orders to fulfil and a tremendous amount of spares would be required to service the huge amount of vehicles that were out on the roads in all parts of the world. On the positive side, all the manufacturing disciplines were in place and had been proven. However, on the negative side there were serious manpower issues. Here we were with an order book as full as any that the company had experienced in recent years, which had to be completed within a relatively short time period.

Now with a settled and trained workforce this manufacturing requirement would have been a difficult enough target to achieve. But then we had to factor in that the company were loosing high numbers of experienced staff who had secured alternative employment in the wake of the pending closure and also allowing people to be transferred to sections of the business that were to continue on the site after the demise of engine manufacture. The only answer available to the company was rather terrifying – and that was to hire temporary staff.

To be honest, this prospect caused me great concern and one or two sleepless nights as well and I initially visualized a total failure in achieving the manufacturing targets set. Would there be enough people out there with the necessary skills to fill the many vacancies that had been created both in shop floor and staff positions? As it turned out, these fears proved to be groundless as the responses that we had from local press advertisements was overwhelming. However, what made it even more pleasing was the fact that many of the temporary people we engaged had worked for us before and had left the company for a variety of reasons, including having been made redundant in earlier lean spells of work.

During that final year of production in 1988, the plant was operating with approximately 50% temporary employees in some key areas. We engaged people as young as 17 and up to retirement age. Indeed it gave me great personal pleasure to interview a 64-year-old Jack Lea who had previously worked for me as a machine tool setter in the 0/500 Engine shop. To say I interviewed him is something of a misnomer. He was such a highly skilled and capable machinist that as soon as he walked into the interview room my only question to him was 'When can you start Jack?' This was also true of other proven ex-employees such as Don Peddie, Bert Kenyon, Dougie Gornall and of course many, many others. Thanks to them and all the other temp's, and not forgetting the permanent staff who saw it through to the bitter conclusion, the end of year target was achieved with a couple of weeks to spare.

Chapter 32 – The Final Farewell

As eventual closure day loomed ever closer, there were many organized and impromptu farewell parties staged. Two of the more memorable events included the final 25-year employee award ceremony and the Christmas party that was organized by our Managing Director, Peter Mathison and his senior managers. This party took the form of a free Christmas lunch for all employees and was staged in the works canteen. The room was suitably decorated and as the diners began to tuck into their festive fare, the sound of sleigh bells could be heard approaching the building – and then it appeared – A large Christmassy sleigh in which was seated Father Christmas (Bob Bamford), pulled by two fine horses (Bob Bullen, Trevor Brown, Jim Troop and

Roger Metcalf). The horses were led by 'Frosty The Snowman' himself (Peter Mathison) and this festive entourage was greeted warmly by the delighted diners. There was however a few choice comments made when the identity of the Christmas gang was revealed including advice to the MD as to just where he could stick the carrot that served as his nose.

There is such a thing as a free lunch after all

....

173

Mr Frosty brings in Santa

And the honour of turning the lights out Goes to ticket number…

The second memorable event was the final award ceremony for those employees who had served 25 years with the company. It was a special night for me as well as although I had received my award many years previously, I had been invited to attend to report on the event and to take photos of the proceedings, which were to be published in the final Leyland Engines newsletter. The event was staged at the prestigious Broughton Park Hotel on the outskirts of Preston and the evening consisted of a splendid meal followed by the award presentations that were made by John Gilchrist, the MD of Leyland DAF.

The rest of the evening was spent dancing, drinking and reminiscing with no worries regarding travelling home as the company had provided accommodation for all the award recipients and their partners. It turned out a busy evening for me taking photographs and listening to the many interesting and often amusing anecdotes.

A West Indian gentleman who had worked in the foundry for many years related a tale that really tickled my fancy. I asked him if he had any abiding memories of his time spent in such a challenging environment as the foundry. He told me that he would never forget the pungent odour of molasses from the baking sand cores that mingled with the sweet smell of 'Kit-e-Kat' that came from the ovens provided for the foundry workers to heat their food. I had often heard of this dubious practice in the past but had always doubted its veracity. "So it was true then?" I enquired rather naively. With a wide Caribbean grin he shook his head and said that no self-respecting West Indian would ever eat cheap cat food – but 'Pedigree Chum', well that was a different matter. With that he slapped his thigh and broke into uproarious laughter and with a twinkle in his eye announced that we white boys were so easy to wind up – "Jerk Chicken with rice and peas man – that was our staple diet." We considered printing this little story in our report of the award ceremony but in the end decided against it.

■■

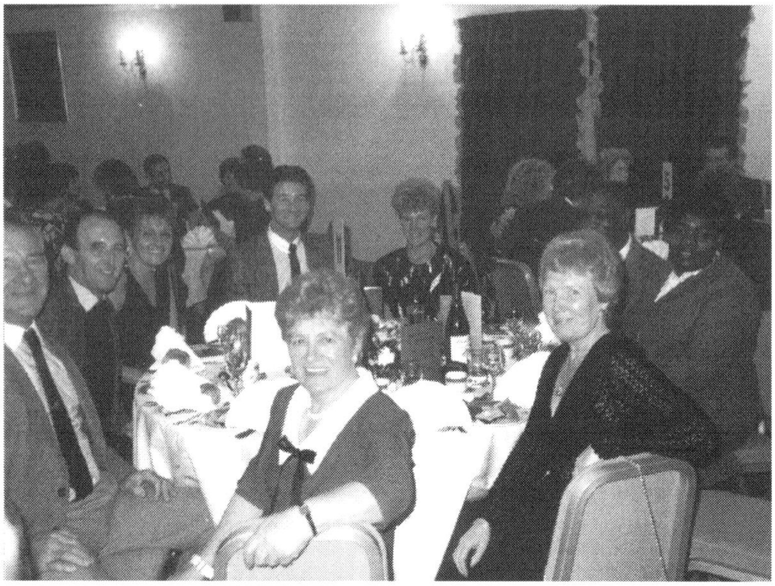

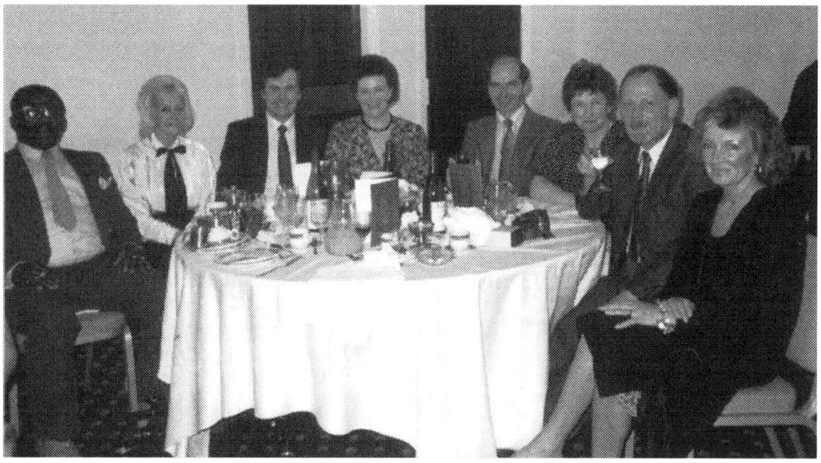

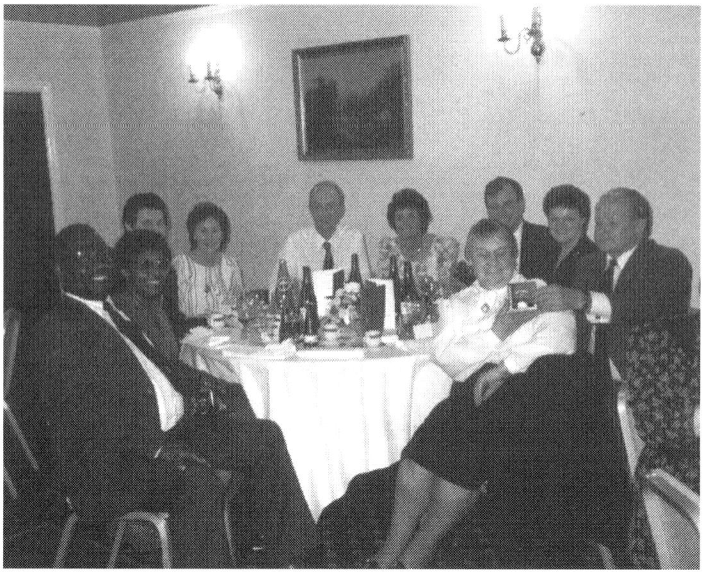

Employees of Leyland Engines enjoying the 25 year awards evening

As the year drew to a close, there were many impromptu farewell parties staged. People were moving on and years of camaraderie and comradeship were now sadly coming to an end. However, they would not be erased or forgotten without that last big 'hurrah' and final farewell. During November and December of 1988 I lost count of the number of farewell 'do's' I attended. You can't work in a company for 38 years without making lots of friends and it would have been unforgivable to part without that final fling – despite the odd furtive tear that was sometimes shed.

■■■

The Final Farewell

It was during these final weeks that one of the people shown in the photograph above decided to investigate what chance we managers had of future employment via the Chinese zodiac signs. It transpired that I was born in the year of the Ox, which meant, according to Chinese philosophy, that I would conquer life through endurance, application, and slow accumulation of energy and that like my fellow oxen I was a genius in the art of meticulous planning; so far so good I thought. However, my ego was somewhat deflated when I read that Oxen can also be extremely authoritarian and pathologically stubborn and prone to obsessive-compulsive personality and schizoid personality disorders. Somehow I didn't think that those final disclosures would look particularly good on my CV.

This revelation quite amused my fellow area manager, Bob Jones, especially when he was informed that he was a Tiger. Surely this marked him out to be a person that would undoubtedly possess all the attributes of the well-known big cat – wouldn't it? Well it started off reasonably enough when he learned that Tigers were fearless in their pursuit of humanitarian causes, were idealistic though somewhat impulsive. That they follow the beat of their own drum, are defiant against injustice, possess large amounts of physical affection and are loyal supporters for just causes. They are also productive, enthusiastic, independent, engaging, dynamic and honourable. The wide grin across Bob's face slowly faded as the assessment continued thus. However, they can also be rash, rebellious, quarrelsome, hotheaded, reckless, anxious, moody, disagreeable, and stubborn. At their worst they can be paranoid, possess histrionic personality disorder and display antisocial tendencies. I threw a comforting arm around Bob's shoulder whilst informing him that if the meanings were to be believed, it looked like we would both be 'signing on' for the foreseeable future.

This little story though has quite an amusing ending. During the final week of operations, the sign shown below was affixed to our office door. I think perhaps the 'Two Ronnies' pinched it from us – or was it the other way round?

> FROM BUFFALO BILL
> &
> TIGER TIM
> ITS GOODBYE FROM ME
> AND GOODBYE FROM HIM!

My role in assisting Jock Gallagher in producing the Leyland Engines Newsletter continued to give me a great deal of pleasure and satisfaction. Although it took up an increasing amount of my managerial duties I considered it as a labour of love rather than a duty. I was taking more and more photographs and reporting on events that were to highlight that final year and although most found their way into the Newsletter, I believed a more permanent reminder ought to be considered to mark this final phase of manufacturing in the plant.

I approached our MD, Peter Mathison and put to him the idea of producing an official album of all the photos that had been taken in the run up to the plant closure. Not only did he approve the idea, he also tasked me to produce not one album but one for every member of the middle and senior management team. Can you imagine the wide smiles that wreathed the faces of the local photographic shop staff when I informed them of this requirement for a minimum of 25 albums? This was further enhanced when it was realized that it would take three volumes of their largest album to hold all the photos that had been taken.

The albums were duly produced and presented to the delighted recipients and I have no doubts that although the years may pass, the pages may yellow and the photos, unlike the million happy memories may fade – yet those well-thumbed pages will continue to turn, each one rekindling many happy recollections of days that are sadly no more…

As I mentioned previously, the company had two specific aims in those final few months. The obvious one was to meet the production targets by the end of 1988, the other was to do all possible to ensure that the workforce were given every opportunity to find alternative employment during this period. The Leyland Assembly Plant took on a number of employees, others found alternative employment through their own efforts and for those remaining a 'Job Shop' was set up which was responsible for finding positions for a great number of employees who otherwise would have remained jobless.

I myself took advantage of the Job Shop and though they managed to secure a couple of interviews for me it appeared that no one wanted to hire a manager with years of front line experience but no academic qualifications other than an ONC and so I resigned myself to lowering my employment sights. With the help of the Job Shop I created a rather impressive CV which I sent to virtually every engineering concern within a 50-mile radius and sat back waiting for the responses to come rolling in. It is sad to report that 90% of the companies sounded did not even extend to me the courtesy of a response; those that did were of the 'Dear John' variety. Just as despair was raising its ugly head I received a phone call – A call that hopefully would lead me to my next position.

The Last Leyland Engine Block Ready For Final Assembly

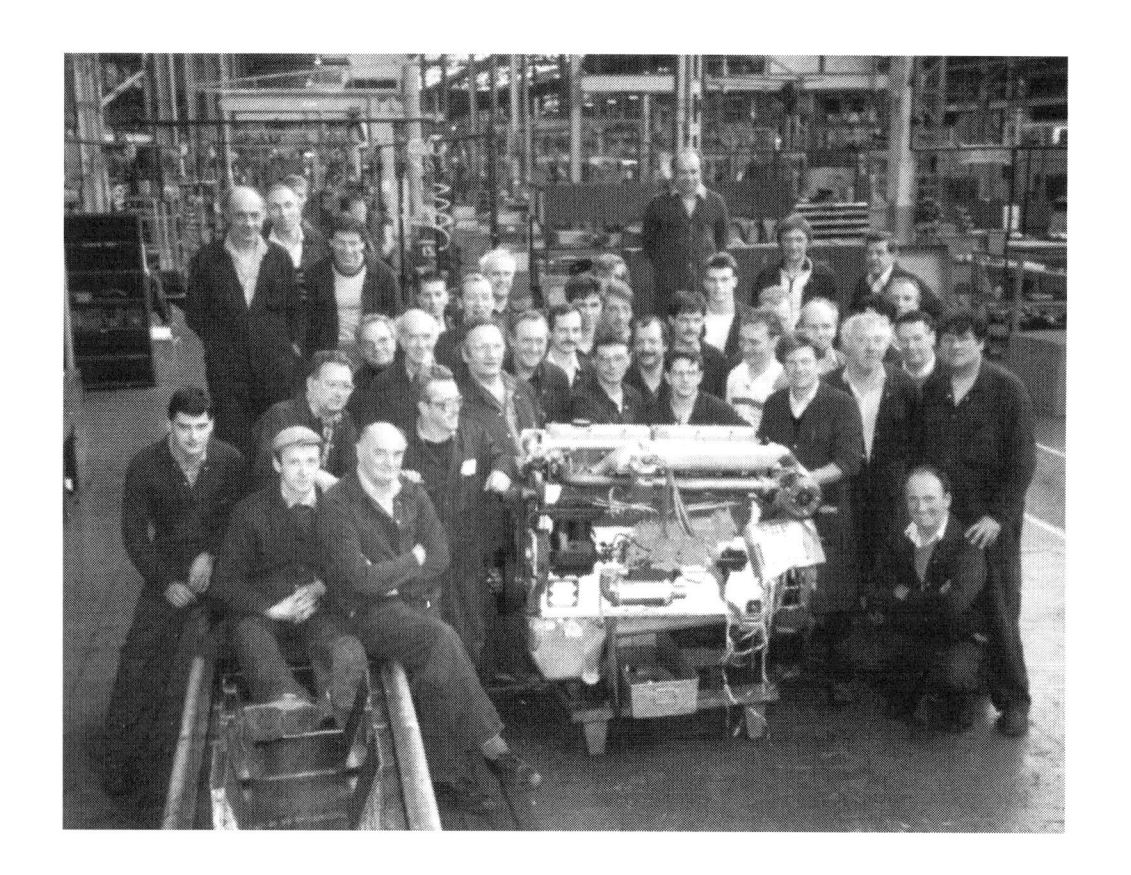

A Fine Bunch Of Men With The Last Of A Fine Product

BOOK 2

Chapter 1 – Full Circle

I think it is fair to relate that this was not my first venture into the world of bus manufacture. Up to the late 1980's Leyland Motors, now operating under the ROVER banner, were in the business of manufacturing both trucks and buses, which meant that up to this date I had an equal involvement in both areas of production. However, as I mentioned in an earlier chapter, 1987 saw the two 'divorced', with the bus empire being taken over initially through a management buyout, which in turn was taken over by the Swedish bus company VOLVO. It was just a year later that truck production was taken over by the Dutch manufacturer DAF.

How then did I manage to return to a company now run by VOLVO? There were two particular reasons for this stroke of good fortune. The first reason concerns my old work colleague Dean Bell, whose footsteps I seemed to have followed since the 1950's. Dean had been appointed works manager of this new concern, which was based on the old Farington manufacturing site, with much of the machining taking place in what had previously been the Comet Shop. Dean was aware of the success achieved by Leyland Engines on the quality front based on the 'Crosby' philosophy and was also aware of the small part that I played in achieving this success. This brings us nicely then to the second reason that initiated my return to bus manufacture.

Towards the end of my time with Leyland Engines and having accomplished little success with the numerous job applications that I had made, I received a somewhat surprising phone call from Dean who made it known that the company would like to know more about the Crosby quality concept and would I be interested in making a presentation to the VOLVO management on its possible merits for the company. My immediate response was that I would be delighted to be given an opportunity to conduct such a presentation and would be even more delighted to assist in implementing the concept within the factory.

The presentation was duly made and I guess I must have said all the right things as within the week I was offered a temporary contract to assist in the possibility of introducing the zero defect concept to VOLVO Bus. The first few weeks with the company were spent in giving quality presentations to various departmental heads and their respective staffs. I sensed that these more tailored presentations were not as enthusiastically received, as was the initial effort with directors and senior management. It was whilst giving one of these seminars to the foremen and first line supervisors that I came to understand this reticence towards the Crosby Quality concept at VOLVO. This was brought home when at the end of the session I was asked why, if it was such a successful concept then how come Leyland Engines had gone to the wall?

In a way I suppose it was a reasonable enough question to ask. However, I think it would be fair to say that if the good Lord himself had come down and performed one of his miracles it would have been in vain. The death knell of Leyland Engines had sounded many months before the Crosby concept had been introduced as I explained in an earlier chapter. Maybe it had bought us a little time but it could never have staved off the inevitable closure of the plant. From that day on, all future presentations opened with me attempting to convince the attendees that linking Crosby with Leyland Engine's demise was flawed logic. The more important objective was to view it not in the shadow of one failed company but rather in the light of the many national and international companies who had adopted the principles enshrined and had then reaped the many benefits that ultimately ensued.

Slowly but surely I sensed a see change among the majority of the workforce and somewhat surprisingly this shift was most apparent among the shop floor operatives. They came to realize that if the concept were to be introduced they would be expected to play a far more active and constructive role regarding manufacturing processes than ever before – and they liked the idea.

There were however, other important elements to put in place before a successful quality procedure could be introduced. These were Plant Operating Procedures and Work Instructions. Now I am not suggesting that these elements did not exist within the company but they had evolved piecemeal over time and were in some cases vague and in others contradictory. Fortunately, I had 'rescued' from the rubbish skip the majority of the Leyland Engine POP's and WI manuals containing these disciplines and was able to convince senior management that to incorporate or in some cases rewrite the existing regulations in line with the Leyland format would ensure a solid foundation if and when the quality concept was introduced.

The next few months therefore were spent with me as part of a small team looking at and developing POP's and WI's that in their own right would be beneficial to the company and would certainly act as the catalyst for the successful introduction of an achievable zero defect quality procedure. The task went well and everybody was pleased with what was being produced. Although I was still employed on a temporary contract I was hopeful that what I had achieved in my relatively short time at VOLVO would ultimately result in me being employed on a more permanent basis. Dean Bell had hinted that this was a distinct possibility – and then came the worst possible news.

Orders for buses globally were in decline. Everyone hoped that this was a blip and that demand would rise eventually. It was not to be. The situation worsened and it came as no great surprise when it was announced that the company would need to make a number of redundancies in an effort to maintain its viability in the diminishing market place. It was even less of a surprise when the trade union representatives pointed out that it was hardly fair to make permanent staff redundant while there was still a number of temporary employees on the books.

In the light of this turn of events it was inevitable that the introduction of the Crosby Quality concept would be at the best suspended and at the worst dropped from the management plans for the business. This indeed was the path taken, which of course immediately put my position at risk. It was a double whammy. I was on a temporary contract and the union was insisting that such employees should be the first to go.

Couple that situation with the fact that Crosby was now destined to be nothing more than a pipe dream, which made my position with the company mighty precarious. I was duly summoned to the boardroom and quite honestly I could have written the 'Dear John' dismissal myself. I was thanked for my invaluable input, given a superb written reference from Dean and after a month's notice I departed with the company's best wishes and a promise that if the order book situation improved I would certainly be among the first to receive consideration for re-employment – and so with those best wishes still ringing in my ears, I departed the factory to the accompaniment of yet another exit gate clanging to behind me.

■■

BOOK 3

Chapter 1 – Ready for Take-Off

My time spent in the aero industry was rather like the company I worked for – jet propelled and it was no sooner started before the journey was completed. Despite once again sending my CV to virtually every engineering company within a 50-mile radius of my home in Bamber Bridge, the responses I received were less than encouraging. Most of my carefully constructed correspondence was apparently filed in company wastebaskets and the few replies I did receive were of the *'Thank you for your enquiry. However'* variety. It appeared that there were still no employers out there that needed or wanted to employ an engineering manager with few technical and even fewer academic qualifications other than 38 years of experience at the sharp end of the business.

However among the few replies that I did receive was one from Rolls Royce Aero Engines in Barnoldswick; a small town that was just about as far as you can travel eastwards from Bamber Bridge and still be in Lancashire.

Like the other responses it appeared that positions for manufacturing managers were as scarce as rocking horse droppings although they gleaned from my CV that I was a time served turner, for which they just happened to have a vacancy. My initial reaction was unprintable but after a further week or so had past without any meaningful visits from the postman, apart of course from the inevitable bills and demands that incurred further delving into a redundancy settlement that I knew could not last for ever, the letter began to take on greater significance. Could I really afford to be so proud that a return to the 'tools' after a near 30-year break was beneath my dignity? The answer came quickly from 'Her who shall be kept in shoes' and a call to the company confirmed that the position was indeed still available.

I started immediately after the Christmas break in 1990 and after the statutory induction procedure I was escorted to the prototype machine shop by a pleasant young man who was to be my foreman. He gave me a quick tour around the various metal shaping machines and enquired if any looked familiar to me. I stopped beside a small Colchester centre lathe and told him that I had worked on such a lathe in the early days of my apprenticeship at Leyland.

"Well," was the immediate response, "I don't see why we can't start you on something you are relatively familiar with," said my new gaffer. "There's less chance of you loosing a finger that way I suppose," he added, grinning broadly. As I pressed the start button it was as if I had never left the 'duckboard'. 30 odd years just slipped away in the blink of an eye as I positioned the tool to make my first cut into a Rolls Royce aero component.

That first week was one of great satisfaction and contentment after the stresses that only factory and man management can bring. My one and only concern was that shapeless lump of metal in my little lathe that I was about to turn (pun definitely intended) into a thing of beauty that would soon be soaring into the wide blue yonder – little did I realize that such contentment could not last.

"Now then Derek," said the foreman, interrupting my reverie. "I suppose you realize we operate a 3-shift system in the machine shop. What do you fancy for next week; mornings, afternoons or nights?" I was about to inform him that none of the shift patterns held any particular appeal, especially when it entailed a 72 mile round trip from my home to the factory. However, realizing that I was no longer in the loop of decision-making I answered meekly, "Afternoons – If that's OK with you boss?" I believed that this was probably the best of the shift options available as mornings would mean a 4 o'clock awakening and the nightshift was just to painful to even contemplate. It turned out to be not so bad as I discovered that the afternoon shifts were not very popular with my younger workmates who lived locally and was able to maintain this work pattern over the next few weeks by 'offering' to do their afternoon stints…

Chapter 2 – In The Shadow of Pendle

I have no doubt that in the more clement seasons of the year the 36-mile journey from Bamber Bridge to Barnoldswick would be most pleasant. The road I was destined to travel meandered serenely enough through the East Lancashire countryside and no doubt on balmier days afforded panoramic vistas of such notable landmarks as Pendle Hill. Unfortunately, I was destined to make this daily trip in the cold and depressing month of January when old Pendle loomed like an amorphous ugly mass from out the wintery gloom.

I had never quite realized how much the weather conditions could change between my starting point and ultimate destination – and I blame it all on Sawley Brow. This long, straight incline on the A59 road near Clitheroe once terrorised motorists until its post war improvement. The hill now is more of a pussycat for modern vehicles but no matter what the extent of enhancement it underwent it could not hope to diminish the height difference between foot and brow. I cannot tell you this difference in feet between the two but can inform you from first hand experience that a light shower at the bottom in winter was the precursor for a near blizzard at the summit.

In the relatively short time that I was employed at Rolls Royce, I encountered snowy conditions at the top of Sawley Brow on quite a number of occasions. In the main they were fairly light scatterings apart from one very memorable occurrence. I had travelled through heavy rain up to the foot of the dreaded brow and was not surprised to see that this had turned to snow at the summit. As I travelled deeper into the East Lancashire countryside the snow showed no signs of abating. When I finally arrived at the factory car park, I reckoned that it was a good three to four inches deep – and was drifting ominously.

All through my shift I kept glancing out of the window, hoping to see signs that those damned white flakes were dwindling – No such luck, if anything the blizzard had increased in its ferocity. At break time, I, along with other concerned travelling workmates visited the car park to assess the situation and were greeted by a total white expanse, quite shallow in some areas but with drifts up to 7 or 8 feet high – and guess where my car was? Well you would have to guess because it certainly couldn't be seen – it was completely covered – and still the snow fell.

It was at that point that I realized that getting home at the end of the shift would be impossible without the aid of skis, a dog sledge or a miracle. As I spoke with colleagues who lived locally I soon realized that this was not an uncommon occurrence in Barnoldswick during particularly hard winters. I also learned that the company had contingency plans for such emergencies and any employee unable to get home would be put up at local hotels or B & B establishments in the area.

In my case neither of these options transpired. Paul H, a workmate of similar age to myself and with whom I had become quite friendly, offered to put me up for the night. I informed Margaret by telephone of my predicament and jokingly informed her that I would see her next spring. It turned out that Paul and his wife lived in a large house near to the factory and with all their children having flown the nest they had bedrooms to spare. An hour or so later, the snow having now stopped, I was sat at Paul's dining table tucking into a massive 'fry up' provided by his good lady for myself and a couple of other refugees from the storm that Paul had invited home.

Later that night, tucked up in a warm comfortable bed in a pair of borrowed pyjamas, I could hear the relentless roar of the snowploughs as they cleared the snow covered roads and was relieved to learn the following morning that all roads out of town were now passable with care. I thanked Paul and his wife profusely for their hospitality and offers to pay for my enforced board and lodgings were met with firm 'No's' from them both. This gesture, followed by assurances that if ever I were stranded again then I would be more than welcome to stay with them. This kind-hearted act to me was a true indication of the sincere warmth and hospitality that can be found firmly ensconced in the hearts of Lancashire folk…

Chapter 3 – A Change of Direction

Soon after my adventures in the snow came another change of direction in my short sojourn at Rolls Royce when I unexpectedly became a 'fitter'. It transpired that due to absenteeism in the sub-assembly area, they were looking for volunteers from the machine shop to fill the breech. When I discovered that this was a regular day job with no shift patterns involved, I reckon I was one of the first in line to offer my services. After an obliging shop steward added the word 'fitter' to my green card I was taken to my new work station and shown my 'fitting' duties which involved nothing more demanding than assembling parts together and tightening a few nuts and bolts – but I certainly was not likely to complain – I was back in the land of the living on regular days.

I was dreading this new job coming to an end as it surely would – and then came my next big career break. Out of the blue, from one of the many companies that I supposed had dismissed my earlier job application came a letter. It was from GEC Alsthom Traction who had a large factory in Strand Road Preston and who manufactured and assembled both traction control equipment and rotating machines (electric motors, generators and auxiliary machines) for the locomotive industry. They had noted from my CV that during my time at Leyland I had spent some time in the Planning department and as they were about to expand their own Manufacturing Planning division, they were looking for engineers with experience in this particular field and would I therefore be interested in coming in for an interview? To darn tooting I would! A job with civilized hours, virtually on the doorstep and with a better financial package than what I was earning with Rolls Royce. Actually GEC Alsthom Traction could have obtained my services for much less but I was hardly likely to tell them so, now was I?

So after 12 interesting and varied weeks in the far flung regions of our great county of Lancashire, I bade my goodbyes to the company and the many friends I had made there in such a relatively short time; picked up my ever-faithful toolbox and on the Ides of March 1990, I headed of to Strand Road in Preston – Hoping that a similar fate, that was to end the career of a famous Roman commander on that auspicious date, was not awaiting me

BOOK 4

Chapter 1 – Final Journey

There is no doubt that fate is a fickle mistress. After a working life to date of 38 years, I now found myself back virtually on my childhood doorstep. I was brought up and went to school not a stones throw away from what was to prove my final employment posting. I knew from the moment that I entered the factory gates that my time with GEC Alsthom Traction, later to be re-branded as ALSTOM, was destined to be enjoyable as I was now back on home ground. This feeling of comfort was further reinforced as my new 'boss', a Mr Ray Cumpstey, gave me a guided tour of the plant and I realized that many of the faces I saw both on the factory floor and in the offices were familiar. It seemed evident that I was not the only expatriate from Leyland Motors who had sought employment at GEC Alsthom Traction from the cheery 'hellos' I received whilst walking through the various departments. It quite amused Mr Cumpstey and he remarked that from the many salutations that were directed at me, I appeared to know more people than he did, despite the fact that he had been employed there for over 30 years.

As I mentioned in the previous chapter, I had been hired as a Manufacturing Planning Engineer and although my previous 'hands on' experience in this particular field of industry had been limited to a short secondment at Leyland, I had garnered enough knowledge to be able to survive the 'honeymoon' period. This coupled with the marvellous help and assistance I received from my fellow planning engineers meant that I quickly established myself as a useful member of the planning team.

The Alstom Planning Team in their new office

However, there was one potential stumbling block to overcome. My previous planning experience at Leyland had been conducted with the aid of pen, pencil, notebook and paper and although GEC Alsthom Traction seemed to be behind Leyland with many of the manufacturing practices, planning procedures were indeed carried out with the aid of computers. Fortunately this proved to be less of a hindrance than I first envisaged, as after an intensive crash course with my mentor, Bob O'Gara, I was soon up to speed with my fellow planners. It was this early introduction to the power and convenience of computing that fostered my love for the discipline that has remained with me to this day.

As my previous background had been with component manufacture and as this was still an integral part of the company's business in the early '90's, I performed the majority of my early planning duties in the main machine shop. I was more than happy as to the direction my new career was taking me, but was acutely aware that the train industry was, like most other manufacturing businesses at the time, very volatile and unpredictable.

Within months of starting at GEC Alsthom Traction I was to experience the first of a number of employment changes that were to pursue me to the very end of my career at the company. The partnership between GEC and Alsthom was becoming more French orientated and in various ways the business was changing and contracting. Manufacturing was then divided into two separate divisions, control equipment and rotating machines and I became a member of the latter under the leadership of Sam Allan, an extremely knowledgeable and popular manager who had worked at the company from leaving school.

A further change to manufacturing policy saw massive reductions of component parts manufactured in-house. This meant that technical planning requirements for such activities were severely reduced and my role, along with many of my planning colleagues took on a more administrative aspect. I was then asked to assist in the fabrication department, which was a totally new venture for me and one that I enjoyed very much – and then along came a major problem – health wise.

My symptoms were quickly diagnosed and I was informed that I had an enlarged prostate gland that required immediate attention. How glad was I that I had joined BUPA, a most welcome fringe benefit that the company were offering at subsidised rates for their employees. Within weeks I had undergone the necessary surgery and was relieved to be told that there were no cancerous cells present in the biopsy. Whilst still recovering I was visited by one of the GEC-Alsthom's nursing staff and asked if I would like to complete my recovery in the company's own convalescent home in Grange-Over-Sand on the fringe of the Lake District. Of course the idea was very appealing but I did not like to think that Margaret would be home alone during this time. Imagine my double delight to be informed that the 10-day convalescent period included partners – and what a great time we had.

Chapter 2 – Convalescing At Hampsfield House

In 1946, Sir George Nelson, a true visionary who was at that time the chairman of English Electric, the forerunner of GEC-Alsthom, founded a convalescent home to allow for the recuperation of his employees after illness. He had purchased a vast Victorian country pile, situated on the outskirts of Grange-Over –Sands and spent many thousands converting it into what was then a state of the art convalescent home. It was originally named in his honour but later became known as Hampsfield House.

Between the opening date and up to its sad closure, many thousands of English Electric employees and indeed employees from subsidiary companies had experienced a rejuvenating period of convalescence in this beautifully appointed home. I was one of those fortunate people and I have to say what a marvellous experience it turned out to be. In all, Margaret and I were privileged to stay at the home on three occasions due to a further prostate procedure and a double hernia and I believe we were in one of the last intakes prior to closure in 2000.

The home itself was cosy without being pretentious. All the staff was superb and saw to our every need. The bedrooms were somewhat old-fashioned with no en-suite facilities but for all that were spacious and comfortable. The various lounges catered for a variety of tastes and preferences and included a billiards room, which was always well patronized. However, I have to say it was the food that made our stay unforgettable. It was not just the quality, which at times bordered on cordon bleu, but also the quantity and the feasting opportunities that made dining so memorable. From waking up to our morning tea to late supper there were six other chances to eat and drink during the day. Breakfast was at 9-00am prompt; a meal that would normally have set me up for the day. Then there was 'elevenses', optional of course but only the strong-willed could resist the tempting trolley. Lunch was served at 1-00pm, again a sumptuous spread that contained enough calories to meet your total daily requirement – and then some. As the clock struck 4-00pm along came the blasted trolley again, groaning with a selection of cakes and other delicacies to die for. The dinner gong sounded at 6-30pm and all us 'guests' filed into the beautiful oak-panelled dining room to once more stuff ourselves silly. Now one would expect that our gourmandising for the day was complete! – Not on your Nelly. Come 9.00pm and the rumbling of trolley wheels would be heard once more. Surely that would be it? I can hear you say – Well if you had staggered up to your bedroom before 10-30pm then yes. However, night owls were then faced by matron's beaming face enquiring if anyone fancied a hot chocolate, which was usually accompanied by whatever 'goodies' had been left on the trolley from it's earlier foray. We learned at the end of the week that it was not permitted for any recovering patient to leave Hampsfield House weighing less than when they first arrived. And I can assure you that unless you were either anorexic or your body harboured a nest of intestinal worms then to lose weight was nigh on impossible.

The House was situated at the end of a half-mile drive from the road and was surrounded by exquisite countryside, including an acre or so of more formal gardens around the house itself. It became something of a ritual for most of the patrons to take a morning stroll around the gardens, mainly in an effort to work up something of an appetite to face the coming days repast. Much of the garden area had seen better days including the walled garden where in years past all the vegetables for the houseguests had been grown. The one area however that was still lovingly tended was the huge side lawn and flowerbeds. If you were lucky enough to be convalescing in the flowering season then the garden was truly a sight to behold. Not only that but part of the lush green sward had been turned into a 9-hole putting green that also doubled as a croquet lawn that on fine days was like a magnet to the more energetic guests.

Chapter 3 – A Walk on the Fell

Just over a rustic stile from the walled garden was a well-trodden field path that led up through Eggerslack Woods and eventually onto Hampsfell and the famous Hospice. Apparently this sturdy shelter had been commissioned and built by a former vicar of Grange-Over-Sands in the 1840's. There are magnificent views from the roof of the building and on a clear day one can see Morecambe Bay and many of the well-known Lakeland peaks such as Helvelyn, Coniston Old Man and the Langdales. There is an intriguing Greek inscription over one of the Hospice doorways, 'RODODAKTYLOS EOS'. Apparently it means 'Rosy Fingered Dawn', which is appropriate I suppose as the doorway does face east. When one of our party heard this translation he remarked, "Poppycock! I think it's more likely to be graffiti put up by a visiting lesbian couple." Naughty boy – However his salacious interpretation did make us all laugh.

Another rather unique feature of a walk on the fell is the limestone pavement leading up to the Hospice. This plateau of limestone rock is now protected but for many years the area was quarried for its lime deposits for both agricultural and building purposes. Evidence of this can still be seen in the number of old limekilns that are dotted about the area, the newer ones still pretty intact. However, some of the really old ones were nothing more than small furnaces built into the hillside.

I was so fascinated by this rather unique geographical area that I visited it many times during my trio of sojourns at Hampsfield House. On one memorable occasion I had risen about 6-00am with the sun streaming through the bedroom window. As I reached the fringe of Eggerslack Woods a most unusual sight confronted me. The ground in front of me was covered with fungi. Being a 'townie' I sincerely hoped that they were of the edible variety as I picked as many as I could carry. I hurried back to the house kitchen and was relieved when cook informed me that they were indeed field mushrooms. She gave me a large basket and I hurried back to what I considered to be the 'mother lode'. I eventually staggered home with the basket full to overflowing. I reckon there were enough mushrooms to last the house for many days – And by golly they were tasty as well.

There were many other opportunities to sally forth from the house, even if it was just to escape that seemingly ever-present tea trolley. Not only could you choose to do your own thing but also there were daily trips out in the house minibus. Every morning the bus would take the houseguests into Grange and bring them back in time for lunch. There were also longer trips out to places like Windermere, Ulverston and Kendal, which were thoroughly enjoyed by all. Alcoholic beverages were not allowed in the house but this did not mean that you were obliged to remain teetotal for the duration of your convalescence, as most evenings the bus would visit one of the many hostelries in the area and a couple of hours of sampling the local brew did wonders for our recovery – or so it seemed at the time. It was after these sessions that the sight of the ubiquitous trolley became more of a treat than a trial.

If my fond experience of 10 days convalescence at Hampsfield House is a sentiment shared by the many hundreds that passed through its welcoming doors then the good Sir George has been justly rewarded by his elevation to the peerage. If memory falters and I forget everything else about my twelve years working with the company, my happy times spent at Hampsfield House will remain an indelible memory forever.

Chapter 4 – Back to Reality

Totally refreshed from my final visit I returned to my post at GEC-Alsthom. However, from then on the business seemed to be in a continuous state of change with redundancies or the threat of them being constant companions of the work force. In June 1998 the company was floated and changed to the simpler, single name of ALSTOM. The business appeared to be in a permanent state of contraction and in 1998/9, as part of yet another rationalisation, the business was further contracted with the eventual closing of all activities at Trafford Park with the remaining business being concentrated at Preston or transferred to sites in France.

Up to date I had been fortunate in managing to maintain my employment with the company but not without one or two 'scares'. The duties of the planning engineers took on various forms and new techniques had to be learned. However I admit that I enjoyed the buzz that these new challenges presented – That is until the time when a new head of department was appointed.

Now it has never been in my nature to be disrespectful and after many years in a managerial position where I met and worked with a variety of fellow managers, I think I can safely say I can recognize the attributes necessary for a person to be a successful manager. By the same token I believe I can also identify the shortcomings that would likewise label an incompetent one. Unfortunately I found few of the former qualities and far to many of the latter in the man who was to be my new boss.

From my own experiences I know that most managers have a great desire to establish good working relationships with their staff at the earliest opportunity; finding out the day to day workings of their new 'empire' and in general familiarising themselves with the people and what makes the department tick. Unfortunately, our 'new broom' came with a preconceived agenda and a host of new policies. Regrettably many of the policies that he attempted to introduce were flawed and impracticable in the industrial climate that was prevalent at that time. When these concerns were discussed with the manager in a calm though resolute manner he seemed to view it as bordering on mutiny, even when issue after issue was proven to be inoperable. I must admit that probably due to my earlier management experience, my contributions to the section meetings that ensued were significant but I believe, always constructive, although on reflection in the manager's eyes it marked me as the 'Fletcher Christian' of this perceived mutiny.

A classic example of his controversial decision-making was evident when a plant wide survey was held in which job titles and salary scales were investigated and rationalized. It came as no great surprise to us Planners on Rotating Machines and Motors when we discovered that that whilst the current job title remained, on advice from our manager we were placed in a lower salary band than our colleagues in the Control Case department, who were performing an almost identical function to our own. When the manager's attention was drawn to this anomaly, his argument that the functions were not the same were quickly and efficiently 'shot down', or so I thought, when I presented him with the job descriptions for both functions – They were virtually identical. Not to be outdone he proclaimed that the job descriptions needed to be re-assessed as in his opinion they were not the same. However, until this was done he proposed to 'red ring' our positions as Planners.

You may be wondering as to just what this 'red ringing' was and how it was applied? Well, it was a way of safeguarding an employee's financial position until the issue in question was fully resolved. Without going into too much detail, I spent many hours of my own time, coupled with assistance from planning engineers in both sections, composing a document to illustrate that the job requirement of planners in both sections was indeed more or less identical. This document was presented to the Human Resources department and we waited anxiously for the outcome. Within days our manager summoned the section to a meeting where he informed us that after due consideration he accepted that both planning functions were 'somewhat similar'. However the look that he gave me as we dispersed that day would have sent chills down the spine of a lesser man. I knew from that moment that my card was well and truly marked.

I think I probably inflamed the situation somewhat when I wrote a little 'blues' number highlighting the shortcomings of this 'red ringing' escapade that was meant to have limited circulation among the planning engineers. Somehow a transcript of it fell into the 'wrong' hands and within a matter of hours there was a copy of it attached to every notice board in the factory. I can just tell that you're all itching to know how the little ditty went – Well, I believe enough water has passed under the proverbial bridge to publish it once more – so here goes:-

Red Ringed Blues (Or the Planner's Lament)

I woke up late, body in pain, Car wouldn't start so I'm late again. Found a big hole in my blue suede shoes, then they hit me with the news. I got those sick and sighing; feel like crying, knocked down RED RINGED BLUES.

Do the work of two men, sometimes three. Reckon the firm don't care for me. My woman's in rags, no food for the kids. Reckon Pete and me are under the skids/ I got those sick of trying; feel like dying, knocked down RED RINGED BLUES.

So what we gotta do to move a grade? We'd ask the boss but we're both afraid. He'd only push us further down, and our RED RINGED BLUES could finish up BROWN! Got them good and plenty, my wallet's empty, knocked down RED RINGED BLUES.

The next few months were somewhat traumatic yet the department continued to play its part in providing planning support for the plant but more in spite of rather than because of the manager's input – And then a further bombshell - Redundancy! Although the final rationalization of the company resulted in the Preston operations being saved, it came at a cost when significant redundancy numbers were announced.

Chapter 5 – And The Axe Fell – Again!

The announcement came as no great surprise to the workforce when the manpower reduction figures were announced and despite the fact that many employees went voluntary, there was no denying that there would need to be compulsory redundancies in all areas. The big talking points now of course was how the selection process would be decided and more importantly, where would the axe fall?

As I weighed up my chances of survival I quickly realized that if the tried and tested formula of 'last in-first out' were applied then I would surely be in the firing line. As it transpired, and although it figured in the equation, it was not to be the overriding criteria for redundancy selection. I believe that the company realized they were carrying a certain amount of 'dead wood' that they would dearly love to cut out and so they came up with a multi point criteria plan that they believed would achieve this aim. The plan included factors such as Relevant Job Experience; Performance of the Job; Accuracy of Work; Job Flexibility & Versatility; Co-operation; Attendance; Timekeeping and as expected, Continuous Service.

On viewing this listing I spied a chink of light in what I had initially assumed was a dark and foreboding place. I was convinced that my performance in the majority of the criteria listed was at least equal to many of my colleagues and perhaps even better than others. Unfortunately my illusion was to be shattered when it was my turn to meet the manager to be informed as to how he had marked me according to the criteria. From what I recall, I don't think there was one category on which we agreed. Needless to say his assessments were far below what I had expected and I informed him in no uncertain terms that I would be lodging an immediate appeal.

It is perhaps unfortunate that before my appeal was heard I was officially declared redundant and had to clear my desk and leave the company. Having now reached my 62nd year I realized that any hopes of finding employment in the world of engineering lay somewhere between very slim and none. However, I remained reasonably upbeat that my appeal would be successful before my redundancy pay out was exhausted.

Chapter 6 – Reprieved

Within a relatively short time I was instructed to attend an appeal hearing that was to be conducted by a senior member of the HR department and an independent line manager. I had used my 'free' time well and with the help and guidance of my union representative, Dave Wooldridge, I had formulated an objective appeal that met with a few raised eyebrows from the appeals panel. Suffice it to say but the original points allocated to the selection criteria were increased by an amount that resulted in the redundancy decision being reversed. This did not mean instant reinstatement although I was put back on the payroll but had to wait until all other appeals had been heard before I could actually return to work.

It took three months for this to happen and as I was now receiving my normal salary, backdated to the start of my redundancy date, I decided to invest the bulk of this payment in to Premium Bonds. I would love to be able to report that I won a million during the investment period but unfortunately it was not to be – but there was always that chance. However, I knew that the money was safe and easily accessed when the time came to repay it.

Finally I was given a date to start the second phase of my employment with the company. I was still to be involved with planning functions but fortunately under the control of yet another manager, who although new to the position possessed all the management skills and attributes so sadly lacking in my previous boss. At the time he was taking a degree course in business studies and knowing of my background in management with my previous employer, he enlisted my assistance in helping compose his dissertation. This I undertook willingly and thoroughly enjoyed the experience. The final results were mutually beneficial as he gained his degree and I was happy to utilise and awaken my latent expertise in creative writing.

Now it wouldn't have been ALSTOM without there being yet another reshuffle in the structure of the business. My previous planning involvement had included component manufacture and the assembly of rotating machines and motors. The decline in this side of the business resulted in me being made part of a team responsible for the procurement and assembly of locomotive traction control equipment. This proved to be the most satisfactory period of my employment with the company as it involved not only working for a first class and progressive manager but also incorporated every aspect of manufacture from the initial design concept to producing the finished customer product. A visiting dignitary once asked me as to how I viewed my position within the team. My reply was along the lines of 'We turn designer dreams into practical realities', which I believe summed up our team's contribution pretty well.

The design team's dream electric motor becomes a reality

I was to remain a member of this team up to the time of my retirement from the company, which unfortunately came a little earlier than I had anticipated. In my social life I was still playing tennis at a reasonably competitive level when quite suddenly I developed a physical condition that reduced my mobility considerably. At first I had thought that the debilitating condition was due to advancing years but when my lack of pace was accompanied by quite excruciating pain I realized that my condition was something rather more sinister than TMB (To Many Birthdays).

A visit to my GP was quickly followed by an appointment with a specialist at the local hospital. After a thorough examination he informed me that I had probably developed a condition known as Lumbar Canal Stenosis and that a neurological test and a CT scan would more than likely confirm his initial opinion. The results of these procedures indicated that the diagnosis had been correct and that I was indeed suffering from a fairly advanced form of LCS. Now I do not intend to bore you any longer than necessary with the details of the condition. Suffice it to say that it resulted in an entrapment of nerves that was causing both the mobility and pain problems and that surgery was now the only option available to me.

It was somewhat disconcerting however to learn that although the prognosis had been speedy and accurate, I would have to wait anything up to 18 months for the required surgical procedure. I would then require anything up to 6 months recuperation before a return to work could even be contemplated. As I was now 63, I did not fancy the idea of having to return to work for a relatively short time after the convalescence period – But this is where the company played a 'blinder'.

It was agreed with my manager and the Human Resources department that if I worked extra hours between now and the date of my operation then I would not have to return to work after the event. This was somewhat radical for such a large company but nevertheless most welcome. The upshot of this was that I was allowed to retire six months prior to my 65th birthday whilst still being on the payroll until I reached this momentous milestone. It all worked out very well as I did indeed have my operation to relieve the trapped nerves without having the worry of knowing that I would have to return to work.

On the allotted day I had a wonderful send off and received a number of very useful retirement gifts. All my previous managers apart from one attended the retirement presentation and there are no prizes for guessing whom the absentee was. I had spent over 12 mostly happy years with ALSTOM and I believe that this was reflected in my valedictory address.

However, this momentous day was not only the end of my time with ALSTOM but it also marked the end of my working life. I had worked with Trucks, Buses, Planes and Trains and do not regret one minute of the 50 years I spent in the manufacturing industry. I learned much and made many dear friends and am now enjoying my time as a free spirit and can only hope that there are many more years left to enjoy the fruits of my retirement.

Barrie Crompton wishes me a happy retirement 2002

The Final Chapter – Comrades Still

Over the 38 happy years that I spent at Leyland Motors, I met a multitude of fine upstanding people, many of who became firm social friends as well as work colleagues. None more so than the comrades in arms and their respective partners that I was fortunate to meet up with during my time working in the Comet Shop. Although we are all now long retired and living in different parts of the county, so firm is the camaraderie between us that periodically we meet up for a nice meal, a few drinks and most important of all, a good 'natter'. Sadly, not all members of the happy band are still with us and as we meet three or four times a year at the various venues, our first toast of the evening is always to – Absent friends.

Printed in Great Britain
by Amazon